VOLUME 2

progress of the world's women 2002

Gender Equality and the Millennium Development Goals

UNIFEM BIENNIAL REPORT

CONTENTS

Acknowledgements

Preface Noeleen Heyzer

1 | **Introduction: Progress of the World's Women**

11 | **Section I: Assessing Progress in Achieving Gender Equality**

55 | **Section II: Innovations in Measuring and Monitoring**

63 | **Conclusion: Moving Forward**

65 | **Technical Notes**

67 | **References**

Charts:

16 — Chart 1 - Secondary Level Enrolment, Ratio of Female Rate to Male Rate, 1999/2000
22 — Chart 2 - Ratio of Female Youth Literacy Rate to Male Youth Literacy Rate, 2002
26 — Chart 3 - Changes in Female Youth Literacy Rate, 1995-2002
34 — Chart 4 - Changes in Female Share of Wage Employment in Non-Agricultural Sector, Early 1980s, Mid-1990s, Latest Available Data
44 — Chart 5 - Changes in Women's Share of Seats in National Parliament, 1987-2000-2002
59 — Chart 6 - Distribution of Total Hours Worked in Cuba, by Sex, 2001

Tables:

18 — Table 1 - Female Enrolment in Secondary Education, 1999/2000
24 — Table 2 - Female Youth (ages 15-24) Literacy Rate (%), 2002
29 — Table 3 - Length of Time Needed to Achieve 95% Female Youth Literacy Rate at Current Rates of Change
32 — Table 4 - Female Share of Wage Employment in Non-Agricultural Sector, Latest Available Data
38 — Table 5 - Informal Employment in Non-Agricultural Employment, by Sex, 1994/2000
39 — Table 6 - Wage and Self-Employment in Non-Agricultural Informal Employment, by Sex, 1994/2000
42 — Table 7 - Women's Share of Seats in National Parliament, November 2002
48 — Table 8 - Countries with Highest Levels of Achievement in Gender Equality and Women's Empowerment
48 — Table 9 - Countries with Lowest Levels of Achievement in Gender Equality and Women's Empowerment
49 — Table 10 - Poverty and Economic Growth, by Region
49 — Table 11 - Maternal Mortality, by Region
50 — Table 12 - HIV/AIDS, by Region, 2002
57 — Table 13 - Index of Fulfilled Commitments
58 — Table 14 - Changes in Gender Gaps, 1990-2000
60 — Table 15 - Gender and Poverty in Latin America
61 — Table 16 - Gender and Poverty in India

PROGRESS OF THE WORLD'S WOMEN 2002: VOLUME 2

Authors: Diane Elson with Hande Keklik
Additional Contributions:
Karen Judd, Joanne Sandler
Editor: Gloria Jacobs
Art Director: Kandy Littrell
Photo Editor: Susan Ackerman
Copy Editor: Tina Johnson
Cover photo: Peter Turnley–Corbis
Printer: Kay Printing

ABOUT THE AUTHORS

Diane Elson is a professor in the Department of Sociology and the Human Rights Centre at the University of Essex in the United Kingdom. She was the coordinator of UNIFEM's *Progress of the World's Women 2000* and is an adviser to UNIFEM on gender responsive budgets. She is the author of many papers on gender and development and is a member of the UN MDG Task Force on Education and Gender (Goals 2 and 3).

Hande Keklik is a consultant in the UNIFEM Economic Security and Rights section. She also was a member of the team that prepared *Progress of the World's Women 2000*. She is a Ph.d. candidate at the University of Utah in the United States, researching the care economy with a particular concentration on domestic workers.

ACKNOWLEDGEMENTS

Several people offered advice and technical expertise in creating this picture of the progress of women worldwide. Compiling an up-to-date and comprehensive set of figures has not been an easy task and would not have been possible without the help of Jens Johansen at the United Nations Educational, Social and Cultural Organization (UNESCO), Sophia Lawrence at the International Labour Organization (ILO), Emmanuel Boudard at the Human Development Report Office and Teresa Valdés, coordinator of the Facultad Latinoamericano de Ciencias Sociales (FLACSO) Chile.

The ongoing support of UNIFEM's bi-lateral partners has been essential to publishing *Progress of the World's Women*. The Department for International Development (DfID) of the UK and the Swiss Agency for Development and Cooperation (SDC) have been steadfast supporters of this publication since its inception. Many others, too numerous to name, have contributed by supporting the UNIFEM programmes that generate the inspiration and information upon which this book is based.

In addition, Joanne Sandler, deputy director for Programmes at UNIFEM, has championed and monitored this project since its inception, and provided support and insight through many drafts. Karen Judd and Zazie Schafer, also of UNIFEM, offered criticism and encouragement throughout the process. And finally Noeleen Heyzer, Executive Director of UNIFEM provided important inputs and guidance throughout. Her leadership in the effort to improve women's lives has been an inspiration to all.

PREFACE

In the last decade of the 20th century governments of the world committed themselves to advance gender equality and women's rights in a series of international conferences, including the International Conference on Population and Development (1994), the Fourth World Conference on Women (1995) and the World Summit on Social Development (1995). These commitments were reaffirmed at five-year review meetings and incorporated into the Millennium Development Goals adopted by UN Member States in 2000.

The Millennium Declaration establishes the values that underlie global development. Stating that gender equality is not only a goal in its own right, but is critical to our ability to reach all development goals, the Declaration resolves "to promote gender equality and the empowerment of women as effective ways to combat poverty, hunger and disease and to stimulate development that is truly sustainable."

Any assessment of progress towards gender equality requires an understanding of the context in which our world is currently shaped: economic globalization, national fragmentation and conflict and problems without borders — all with major consequences for women's lives. The financial crises in Asia and Latin America and the world trade negotiations have highlighted the issues that need to be addressed in globalization. While many women have benefited from new opportunities opened by globalization, others have experienced new or deepening inequalities in access to opportunities and resources. We must make globalization work for all women, so that those relegated to badly paid jobs in the informal and casual sectors or struggling for livelihoods in poor, rural areas can benefit.

A parallel process is one of fragmentation, along lines of ethnicity, language and religion. There are more intra-state conflicts today than at any time in recent history. The use of gender-based violence, including rape, forced pregnancy and deliberate infection with HIV/AIDS, has become a horrifying feature of ethnic and religious conflicts. While gains have been made in terms of international frameworks and national plans of action to combat violence against women, it remains one of the most pervasive human rights violations worldwide.

Both globalization and fragmentation have been accompanied by a rise in problems that know no borders, including trafficking in women and children and the continuing spread of HIV/AIDS, a disease which has decimated families and communities, leaving AIDS orphans in the care of women who themselves are ill.

Against this background, it is significant that 189 nations adopted women's empowerment and gender equality as one of the eight Millennium Development Goals. One month after the Millennium Summit, in October 2000, the Security Council adopted Resolution 1325 on Women Peace and Security, which recognized the impact of war on women and included specific recommend-

PREFACE

ations for improving women's protection during conflict and women's leadership in peace-building and reconstruction. And in June 2001, at the UN General Assembly Special Session on HIV/AIDS, nations agreed to a set of targets to promote girls' and women's empowerment as "fundamental elements in the reduction of the vulnerability of women and girls to HIV/AIDS."

These resolutions and documents unite the goals of human development, human security and gender equality. They build upon the commitments to gender equality made at the world conferences of the 1990s and in the Convention on the Elimination of All Forms of Discrimination against Women (CEDAW), which has now been ratified by 171 countries. Nevertheless, they leave critical questions unanswered: What will it take for all the countries and communities of the world to meet these goals? How do we measure gender equality and women's empowerment? How can we prevent the gains of the last decade from being lost in the current world context?

The fact that tracking progress on gender equality and women's rights is on the agenda is, itself, a sign of progress. But for commitments to have an impact, we need accountability, action, and political will. *Progress of the World's Women 2002* is issued at a time when there is a deeply held hope of achieving the Millennium Development Goals and of progress for all people. This hope can be fulfilled only in a world where human rights and human security move from the margins to the centre, to create a safer, better world for all.

Noeleen Heyzer
Executive Director,
UNIFEM

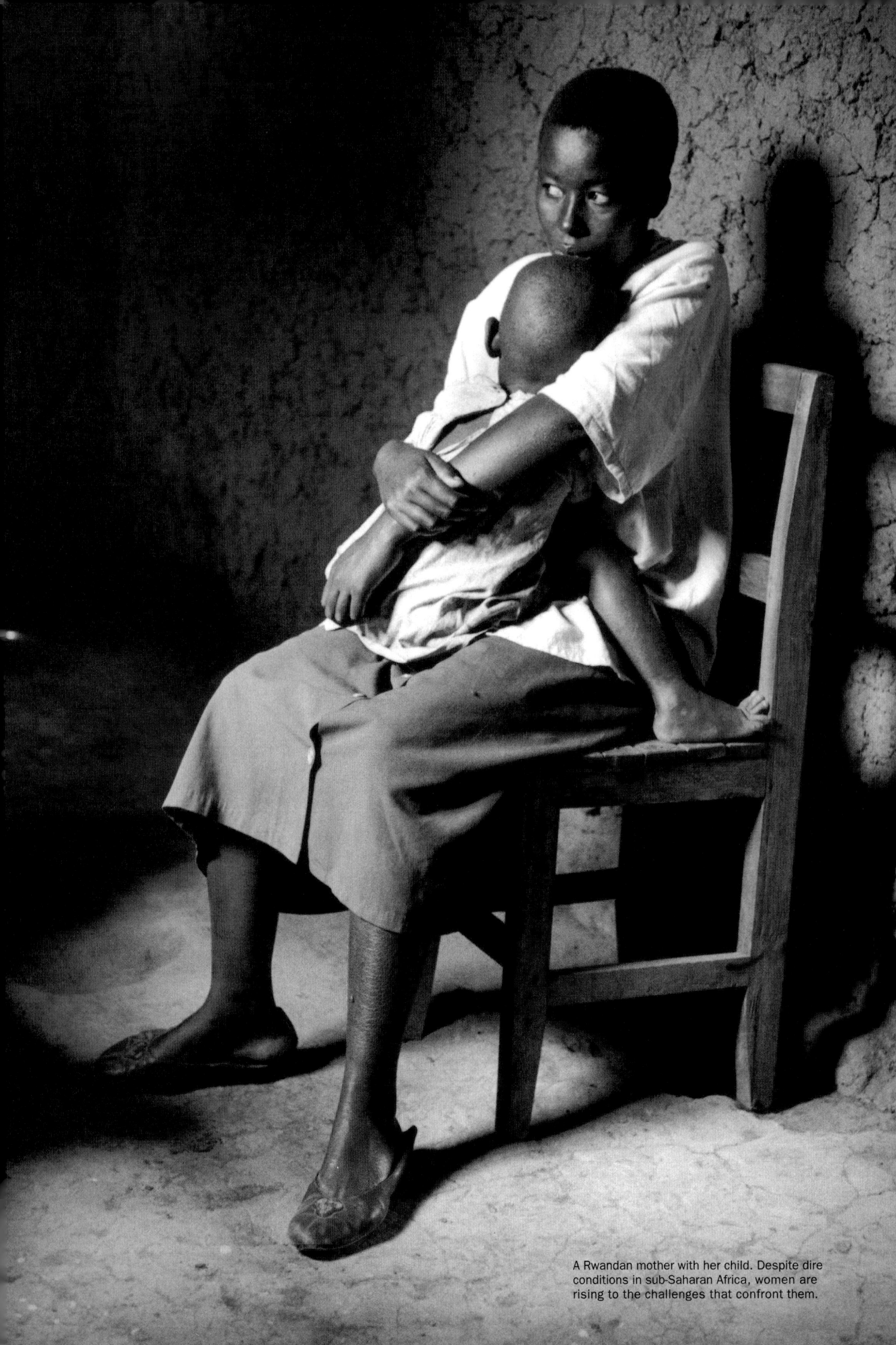

A Rwandan mother with her child. Despite dire conditions in sub-Saharan Africa, women are rising to the challenges that confront them.

INTRODUCTION
GENDER EQUALITY AND THE MILLENNIUM DEVELOPMENT GOALS

progress of the world's women

Progress—the word conjures images of purposeful movement towards a better world; it seems to signify traveling a path to higher ground. Yet there is never a guarantee of progress in any endeavour, nor is its path direct when it does occur. This is as true of progress for women as anything else. The differences in the experiences, expectations and priorities of different groups of women mean that there is always scope for debate about what constitutes progress for them. Moreover, progress in one area does not guarantee progress in all areas: women may enjoy certain rights yet still suffer extreme discrimination. This report, the second edition of *Progress of the World's Women*, explores the challenges of tracking and determining such progress. Its goal is to support efforts to improve the monitoring of and advocacy for implementing the commitments made to women in the world conferences of the 1990s and other global agreements.

The difference between 2002 and 2000, when we last published *Progress of the World's Women*, is that we now have the Millennium Declaration and the Millennium Development Goals (MDGs). These were agreed to in September 2000 when world leaders met at the Millennium Summit at the United Nations. The Millennium Declaration establishes the values that should guide global development — freedom, equality, solidarity, tolerance, respect for nature and shared responsibility — and promises to free "the entire human race from want." In the Declaration leaders pledged to "promote gender equality and the empowerment of women as effective ways to combat poverty, hunger and disease and to stimulate development that is truly sustainable." The Declaration also states, in paragraph 6, that "Men and women have the right to live their lives and raise their children in dignity, free from hunger and from fear of violence, oppression or injustice…" and that "the equal rights and opportunities of women and men must be assured."

The eight Millennium Development Goals (see Box 1) commit world leaders to an ambitious agenda for change. For all of the goals, a set of time-bound targets and indicators have been proposed (see Box 4, p. 8) as a means of tracking progress.

This edition of *Progress* presents data and analysis related to Goal 3 of the MDGs: "promote gender equality and empower women." It is significant that the Millennium Declaration identified gender equality and women's empowerment as a goal in its own right and an essential component in achieving all of the other goals. That world leaders agree that women's equality and rights are central to achieving economic and social priorities is important. It is equally important that these goals are recognized as goals for the entire world — they are neither only for those countries that have achieved a certain level of development nor for those that have yet to do so.

In this report, we review the basis upon which the commitment to gender equality was made and the opportunities and challenges involved in ensuring that written promises are turned into concrete opportunities for women. The main section of the report presents an international cross-country assessment of women's situation at the beginning of the new millennium, using the MDG indicators for Goal 3. This information updates the review undertaken in *Progress 2000*. As before, statistics are at the heart of this work, yet numbers alone cannot capture the rich diversity of

> **Study after study has shown that there is no effective development strategy in which women do not play a central role. When women are fully involved, the benefits can be seen immediately: families are healthier and better fed; their income, savings and reinvestment go up. And what is true of families is also true of communities and, in the long run, of whole countries.**
> **—UN Secretary-General Kofi Annan**
> **March 8, 2003**

women's lives. Many aspects of women's progress — or lack of it — are left out when the focus is on hard facts: the emotional pull of the unpaid care work that women provide in their homes and communities; the excitement and the exhaustion stemming from the struggle for equality and respect; the terrible toll of the ongoing violence that women experience, in public and in private, in war and during peace. With this context in mind, this report recognizes the strength and limits of the indicators chosen to record women's progress. It treats them as information to be used in an ongoing discussion, rather than as facts that close off debate.

The report will demonstrate that, when comparing the different regions of the world, women in sub-Saharan Africa face the greatest challenges. Sub-Saharan Africa has the highest level of maternal deaths and the highest prevalence levels of HIV/AIDS. The majority of HIV positive adults are women. Almost half the population lives on less than US$1 a day, the highest rate of poverty in the world. It is also the region with the lowest per capita gross national product. Average regional income has fallen in the period 1990 to 2000. All of this is reflected in the statistics on MDG indicators: The rates of girls' school enrolment and young women's literacy are low compared to other regions, and compared to boys and men's rates within the region. Women's share of wage employment in the non-agricultural sector is equally low compared to other regions and compared to men. Nevertheless, women in the region are rising to the enormous challenges that confront them. In many countries, they are beginning to play a larger role in decision-making, as members of parliaments and as activists involved in gender budget initiatives.

Given the heated debate about what constitutes progress for women, the second section of the report offers a review of different initiatives being undertaken in countries and regions worldwide to assess progress towards gender equality. It provides examples of a range of innovative attempts to liberate data, build gender-sensitive supplementary indicators and

BOX 1: MILLENNIUM DEVELOPMENT GOALS

Goal 1. Eradicate extreme poverty and hunger
Goal 2. Achieve universal primary education
Goal 3. Promote gender equality and empower women
Goal 4. Reduce child mortality
Goal 5. Improve maternal health
Goal 6. Combat HIV/AIDS, malaria and other diseases
Goal 7. Ensure environmental sustainability
Goal 8. Develop a global partnership for development

make this information available to advocates who can use it to increase accountability and action. This initial review shows that, while the world has agreed on a visionary Millennium Development Goal for gender equality and women's empowerment, there are many intersecting pathways that countries and communities will travel to move from rhetoric to reality.

Finally, it is important to note what this report will not do. While gender equality is central to all of the Millennium Development Goals, this report will not track progress on the gender dimensions of the targets and indicators for the seven other goals. This is a critical task that lies ahead. Gender equality advocates have already taken on the challenge of bringing attention to this and UNIFEM will be supporting and joining these efforts. Likewise, achieving the MDGs is not simply a matter of tracking progress. Rather, it is dependent on developing innovative and sustainable approaches to the issues that the eight goals address. This report does not explore the 'how' of achieving gender equality and women's empowerment. However, it acknowledges that this is the fundamental question that must be answered for the goals to be achieved.

A GLOBAL CONSENSUS ON GENDER EQUALITY AND WOMEN'S HUMAN RIGHTS

It is not by chance that the Millennium Declaration and the MDGs identify gender equality and women's empowerment as central, cross-cutting goals. The work of gender equality advocates over many decades created a groundswell of programmes and plans of action at global, regional and national levels that committed countries to achieving gender equality. The commitments made in the UN world conferences of the 1990s — as well as subsequent UN meetings in early 2000 — are central to the vision embedded in the Millennium Declaration and in Goal 3 of the MDGs. The Fourth World Conference on Women (Beijing, 1995) played an extremely important role. It produced the Beijing Platform for Action (PFA), an ambitious roadmap for achieving gender equality that highlights 12 areas in which action is urgently needed. Other world conferences of the 1990s — including those on human rights (Vienna, 1993), population and development (Cairo, 1994), and the World Social Summit on Development (Copenhagen, 1995) — reiterated the call for women's empowerment and rights. Equally important, 171 countries (as of March 2003) have ratified the UN Convention on the Elimination of All Forms of Discrimination against Women (CEDAW), an international women's bill of rights that obligates governments to take actions to promote and protect the rights of women. It is critical that the spirit and visionary commitments embedded in these documents are not lost as countries and development assistance agencies organize around the set of targets and indicators selected to track progress on the MDGs.

Progress in implementing the PFA and CEDAW also show some of the complexities in achieving Goal 3 and fulfilling all the commitments made to women. The five-year review of progress in implementing the PFA (UN 2001), held in June 2000, showed that the path of progress had been bumpy at best. As the report, *Beijing and Beyond*, states, "New approaches are needed to address [these] opportunities and challenges within the Platform's vision of gender equality and women's empowerment. Specific policy issues concerning women and girls, such as work-related rights, gender-based violence, reproductive and sexual health and rights, education and social security, access to productive resources including credit and nutrition require sustained attention."

The uneven implementation of the PFA results from a complex set of conditions that are at the heart of women's inequality. The structures that perpetuate gender inequality and discrimination pervade economic, social, political, cultural, legal and civic institutions, norms and practices around the world. The know-how and investments required to eliminate these are rarely committed, especially in poor countries. The political will required to achieve gender equality is variable or altogether lacking. Although there are positive and practical examples in almost every country of actions taken that have improved women's status, "significant challenges remain," according to *Beijing and Beyond*.

Progress has also been disappointing in fulfilling commitments to address other social and economic priorities highlighted by the UN world conferences. Governments have pledged to eradicate poverty and environmental degradation, to reverse the spread of HIV/AIDS and other pandemics, to ensure education for all and to promote human and reproductive rights, to name a few of the key priorities. Five-year reviews of these commitments indicate that here too progress has been slow, uneven, and has largely bypassed the poorest and most marginalized sectors of society.

GENDER EQUALITY AND THE MILLENNIUM DEVELOPMENT GOALS

It is in this context of commitments made and not yet fulfilled that the MDGs must be assessed. Programmes and plans of actions that emerged from the different UN world conferences contained a relatively small number of quantitative time-bound targets, many of which were brought together in 1996 by the 21 donor governments of the Organization for Economic Cooperation and Development (OECD) as seven International Development Targets (IDTs). Despite a number of commit- [CONTINUED ON PAGE 6]

BOX 2: INTERNATIONALLY AGREED-UPON TARGETS

Targets	Cairo (ICPD)	Copenhagen (WSSD)	Beijing (FWCW)	Beijing +5	Johannesburg (WSSD+5)	UN GA-Resolution on HIV/AIDS
Governments reiterated the target for women in decision-making positions endorsed by ECOSOC: 30% of decision-making positions to be held by women			PFA182			
Eradicate absolute poverty by a date to be specified by each country		POA25				
By the year 2000, governments committed themselves to meet basic needs:						
Universal access to basic education and completion of primary education by at least 80% of primary school-age children	POA11.6	POA36a	PFA80b			
Gender equality for girls in primary education			PFA81b			
Life expectancy not less than 60 years in any country		POA36b				
Mortality rates of infants and children under 5 reduced by one-third of the 1990 level, or 50 to 70 per 1,000 live births, whichever is less	POA8.16	POA36c	PFA106l			
Maternal mortality reduced by one half of the 1990 level	POA8.21	POA36d	PFA106i			
Severe and moderate malnutrition among children under-5 reduced by half of the 1990 level		POA36f	PFA106w			
Primary health care for all, reducing malaria mortality and morbidity by at least 20% from 1995 levels in at least 75% of affected countries		POA36g				
Eradication or control of major diseases constituting global health problems		POA36j				
Greater availability of affordable and adequate shelter for all		POA36m				
By the year 2005, governments promised to:						
Close the gender gap in primary and secondary education	POA11.8	POA36a	PFA80b			
Remove all programme-related barriers to family-planning	POA7.19					
Countries with intermediate mortality rates aim for infant rate below 50 deaths per 1,000 and under-5 rate below 60 deaths per 1,000 births	POA8.16					
Countries with highest maternal mortality rates aim for a rate below 125 per 100,000 live births; those with intermediate rates aim for a rate below 100	POA8.21					
Countries with highest mortality rates to achieve life expectancy greater than 65; all other countries, a life expectancy greater than 70	POA8.5					
Create and maintain a non-discriminatory and gender-sensitive legal environment by reviewing legislation with a view to removing discriminatory provisions, preferably by 2005, and eliminating legislative gaps that leave women and girls without protection of their rights and without effective recourse against gender-based discrimination				A/RES/S-23/3 68b		
Develop and accelerate the implementation of national strategies that promote the advancement of women and women's human rights, that promote shared responsibility of men and women to ensure safe sex and empower women to have control over matters related to their sexuality to increase their ability to protect themselves from HIV infection						A/RES/S-26/2 59

Targets	Cairo (ICPD)	Copenhagen (WSSD)	Beijing (FWCW)	Beijing +5	Johannesburg (WSSD+5)	UN GA-Resolution on HIV/AIDS
Implement measures to increase capacities of women and adolescent girls to protect themselves from HIV infection, principally through the provision of health care and health services, including sexual and reproductive health, and through prevention education that promotes gender equality						A/RES/S 26/2 60
Ensure development and accelerated implementation of national strategies for women's empowerment, the promotion and protection of women's human rights and reduction of their vulnerability to HIV/AIDS						A/RES/S-26/2 61

By the year 2015, governments promised to:

Targets	Cairo (ICPD)	Copenhagen (WSSD)	Beijing (FWCW)	Beijing +5	Johannesburg (WSSD+5)	UN GA-Resolution on HIV/AIDS
Accelerate action and strengthen political commitment to close the gender gap in primary and secondary education by 2005 and to ensure free compulsory and universal primary education for both boys and girls by 2015, and eliminate policies that worsen and perpetuate the gap				A/RES/S-23/3 67c		
Provide universal primary education in all countries	POA 11.6	POA 36a	PFA 80b			
Achieve an infant mortality rate below 35 per 1,000 live births and an under-5 mortality rate below 45 per 1,000	POA 8.16	POA 36d	PFA 106l			
Make reproductive health care accessible to all individuals of appropriate ages through the primary health-care system	POA 7.6	POA 36h	PFA 106i			
Achieve equivalent levels of education for boys and girls	POA 11.6					
Reduce maternal mortality rates by a further one-half	POA 8.21					
Countries with highest maternal mortality rates aim for a rate below 75 per 100,000 live births; those with intermediate rates aim for a rate below 60	POA 8.21					
Countries with highest mortality rates to achieve life expectancy greater than 70; all other countries, a life expectancy greater than 75	POA 8.5					
Support and strengthen national, regional and international adult literacy programmes with international cooperation in order to achieve a 50 percent improvement in the levels of adult literacy especially for women and equitable access to basic and continuing education for all adults				A/RES/S-23/3 1f		
Reinforce efforts to ensure universal access to high quality primary health care throughout the life cycle, including sexual and reproductive health care, no later than 2015				A/RES/S-23/3 79b		
Reaffirm the internationally agreed development goal of achieving universal primary education, in particular that, by 2015, children everywhere, boys and girls alike, will be able to complete a full course of primary schooling					A/57/532/add1	

PFA : BEIJING PLATFORM FOR ACTION ; POA : PROGRAM OF ACTION ; UN GA : UNITED NATIONS GENERAL ASSEMBLY

[CONTINUED FROM PAGE 3] ments already made to women at the world conferences, the only IDT related to gender equality was one that called on governments to demonstrate "progress toward gender equality and the empowerment of women by eliminating gender disparity in primary and secondary education by 2005."

The eight Millennium Development Goals build on and expand the IDTs. The dates by which specified levels of progress for each of the goals are to be achieved are included in the accompanying 18 targets and 48 indicators (see Box 4, p.8-9). Unlike the IDTs, the MDGs represent a consensus among all the countries of the world, rather than just the OECD nations. Additionally, Goal 8 — "develop a global partnership for development" — is viewed as a promise by donor governments to take on substantive and specific responsibility for helping other countries achieve the goals.

As countries organize to track progress towards achieving the MDGs, there is an opportunity to re-energize gender equality initiatives by insisting on the centrality of Goal 3 and the Millennium Declaration. As a forthcoming World Bank report notes, "Because the MDGs are mutually reinforcing, progress towards one goal affects progress towards others. Success in many of the goals will have positive impacts on gender equality, just as progress toward gender equality will help other goals" (Carlsson and Valdivieso 2003). In this regard, it is absolutely essential to ensure that tracking progress towards all of the eight goals relies on sex-disaggregated data and gender-sensitive indicators. Many agencies and advocates for gender equality — including the United Nations Development Programme (UNDP), the World Bank and numerous academic and non-governmental organizations (NGOs) — are producing reports that will contribute to understanding the gender dimensions of many of the goals and targets.

Growing interest in the MDGs also presents an opportunity to stimulate national and local dialogues about the way in which a country or community wants to achieve the goals. For instance, in the background paper produced by the Millennium Project Task Force for Goal 3, entitled "Promises to Keep," the authors review different interpretations of gender equality:

> The UN's *Human Development Report* (1995) refers to gender inequality in terms of capabilities (education, health, and nutrition) and opportunities (economic and decision-making). Similarly, the World Bank defines gender equality in terms of equality under the law, equality of opportunity (including equality of rewards for work and equality in access to human capital and other productive resources that enable opportunity), and equality of voice (the ability to influence and contribute to the development process)." (Grown et al. 2003:3)

Alongside the importance of debating Goal 3 and incorporating it into public programmes is the recognition that fulfilling it strictly within the confines of the MDGs presents certain problems. This complex goal has been encapsulated into a single target calling for the elimination of gender disparity in primary and secondary education, preferably by 2005, and in all levels of education no later than 2015. Education is important, but as the Beijing Platform for Action recognized, there are many other kinds of gender disparity that are equally important and must be addressed — disparity in the economy, in political life, in family life and in the law, among others.

Fortunately, the indicators for Goal 3 are somewhat broader than the target:
- the ratio of boys to girls in primary, secondary and tertiary education
- the ratio of literate women to men aged 15-24
- the share of women in wage employment in the non-agricultural sector
- the proportion of seats held by women in parliament

Thus achievement of the target for Goal 3 should be treated as a signpost in reaching the goal, not as a substitute for it, and the indicators can be used to fill in additional details. As discussed throughout this report, the empowerment of women does not just depend on the elimination of numerical gender disparities. It is possible to equalize the enrolment of boys and girls in school at a low level for both, a situation that empowers neither. Equality in deprivation does not represent a genuine fulfilment of Goal 3.

> **For UNIFEM, Goal 3 — gender equality and women's empowerment — is the goal through which women's perspectives must be incorporated into all of the other goals, including that of halving the number of people living on less than a $1 a day. If this goal is to be reached it is critical that the feminization of poverty, increasingly recognized by governments as well as international documents, receive systematic attention — especially in this era of globalization.**
> **—Noeleen Heyzer**
> **Executive Director, UNIFEM, 2002**

BOX 3: MAKING GENDER EQUALITY CENTRAL TO ALL THE MDGS

Just as the Beijing Platform for Action and other globally-agreed upon commitments have their greatest impact when taken up as tools for advocacy, so too efforts to implement and track progress on the MDGs will have the most impact when they are translated into locally relevant strategies and monitoring efforts. This is where the real challenges and opportunities lie. It is essential that advocates for gender equality and women's rights participate fully in shaping and influencing the strategies for achieving the MDGs at local and national levels.

What are the opportunities for ensuring that the MDGs reinforce commitments already made to women? Some ideas:

1. *Ensure that national MDG reports take national commitments to women into account.* More than 40 countries have already produced Millennium Development Goal Reports (MDGRs) and it is expected that most countries will do this on an annual basis. Thus far, the record of incorporating gender equality and women's rights into the MDGRs has not been encouraging, and women's voices are notably lacking from most efforts. Women's rights advocates must participate in the efforts to identify country-specific targets and indicators that will track progress in ways that take both women and men into account. Some positive examples do exist. In the Viet Nam MDGR the country used its National Plan of Action for the Advancement of Women as the basis for identifying targets and indicators towards achievement of Goal 3 and thus included reduction in the rate of violence against women as a target.

2. *Improve the data collection and analysis upon which MDG tracking is based.* It is widely acknowledged that there are significant challenges related to the statistics and indicators that are available for tracking progress. In the poorest countries — but also in many others — the systems and skills needed to generate and analyse sex-disaggregated data are in short supply. In many countries, even where the data exists, it is not used. While national and local level monitoring are the only guarantee that a true picture of women's achievements will emerge, there is still insufficient data to generate information that can be easily compared and contrasted. As research on the MDGs gets underway, the shortcomings of the data are ever more apparent. It is absolutely essential that countries — especially poor countries — receive support to improve their ability to collect, produce and use gender-disaggregated data. Many efforts have been launched in this regard (see pp. 55-61), but a worldwide effort and local level advocacy is imperative if the analysis upon which MDG reports are based is to truly reflect progress towards gender equality.

3. *Document and publicize success.* While tracking progress has great value, it is even more important to track, implement and learn from all the innovative strategies developed by people and organizations the world over that actually bring countries closer to the goal of gender equality. Achieving the MDGs will require that these practices and innovations become common practice. Gender equality advocates have a key role to play in bringing these innovations into the mainstream and pressuring governments to ensure that knowledge about what works — and what does not — informs national and local level strategies to achieve the MDGs.

BOX 4: MDG GOALS, TARGETS AND INDICATORS

Goal 1. Eradicate extreme poverty and hunger
Target 1. Halve, between 1990 and 2015, the proportion of people whose income is less than one dollar a day
Indicators
1. Proportion of population below $1 (PPP) per day (World Bank*)
2. Poverty gap ratio (incidence x depth of poverty) (World Bank)
3. Share of poorest quintile in national consumption (World Bank)

Target 2. Halve, between 1990 and 2015, the proportion of people who suffer from hunger
Indicators
4. Prevalence of underweight children under five years of age (UNICEF, WHO)
5. Proportion of population below minimum level of dietary energy consumption (FAO)

Goal 2. Achieve universal primary education
Target 3. Ensure that, by 2015, children everywhere, boys and girls alike, will be able to complete a full course of primary schooling
Indicators (UNESCO)
6. Net enrolment ratio in primary education, girls, boys, total
7. Proportion of pupils starting grade 1 who reach grade 5 (girls, boys, total)
8. Literacy rate of 15- to 24-year-olds, women, men, total

Goal 3. Promote gender equality and empower women
Target 4. Eliminate gender disparity in primary and secondary education, preferably by 2005, and to all levels of education no later than 2015
Indicators
9. Ratio of girls to boys in primary, secondary and tertiary education (UNESCO)
10. Ratio of literate women to men of 15- to 24-year-olds (UNESCO)
11. Share of women in wage employment in the non-agricultural sector (ILO)
12. Proportion of seats held by women in national parliament (IPU)

Goal 4. Reduce child mortality
Target 5. Reduce by two thirds, between 1990 and 2015, the under-five mortality rate
Indicators
13. Under-five mortality rate (UNICEF, WHO)
14. Infant mortality rate (UNICEF, WHO)
15. Proportion of 1-year-old children immunized against measles (UNICEF, WHO)

Goal 5. Improve maternal health
Target 6. Reduce by three quarters, between 1990 and 2015, the maternal mortality ratio
Indicators
16. Maternal mortality ratio (UNICEF, WHO)
17. Proportion of births attended by skilled health personnel (UNICEF, WHO)

Goal 6. Combat HIV/AIDS, malaria and other diseases
Target 7. Have halted by 2015 and begun to reverse the spread of HIV/AIDS
Indicators
18. HIV prevalence among 15-to-24-year-old pregnant women (UNAIDS, UNICEF, WHO)
19. Condom use rate of the contraceptive prevalence rate (UNICEF, UN)
20. Number of children orphaned by HIV/AIDS (UNICEF, UNAIDS)

Target 8. Have halted by 2015 and begun to reverse the incidence of malaria and other major diseases
Indicators
21. Prevalence and death rates associated with malaria (WHO)
22. Proportion of population in malaria risk areas using effective malaria prevention and treatment measures (UNICEF, WHO)
23. Prevalence and death rates associated with tuberculosis (WHO)
24. Proportion of tuberculosis cases detected and cured under directly observed treatment short course (DOTS, WHO)

Goal 7. Ensure environmental sustainability
Target 9. Integrate the principles of sustainable development into country policies and programmes and reverse the loss of environmental resources
Indicators
25. Proportion of land area covered by forest (FAO)
26. Ratio of area protected to maintain biological diversity to surface area (UNEP, IUCN)
27. Energy use (kg oil equivalent) per $1 GDP (PPP) (IEA, UNSD, World Bank)
28. Carbon dioxide emissions (per capita) (UNFCCC, UNSD) and consumption of ozone-depleting CFCs (ODP tons) (UNEP-Ozone Secretariat)
29. Proportion of population using solid fuels (WHO) (not yet available)

Target 10. Halve by 2015 the proportion of people without sustainable access to safe drinking water

Indicator
30. Proportion of population with sustainable access to an improved water source, urban and rural (UNICEF, WHO)
Target 11. By 2020 to have achieved a significant improvement in the lives of at least 100 million slum dwellers
Indicators
31. Proportion of urban population with access to improved sanitation (UNICEF, WHO)
32. Proportion of households with access to secure tenure (owned or rented) (HABITAT)

Goal 8. Develop a global partnership for development
[Indicators for targets 12-15 are given below in a combined list.]
Target 12. Develop further an open, rule-based, predictable, non-discriminatory trading and financial system.
Includes a commitment to good governance, development, and poverty reduction — both nationally and internationally
Target 13. Address the special needs of the least developed countries.
Includes: tariff and quota-free access for least-developed countries' exports; enhanced programme of debt relief for HIPCs and cancellation of official bilateral debt; and more generous ODA for countries committed to poverty reduction
Target 14. Address the special needs of landlocked countries and small island developing States (through the Programme of Action for the Sustainable Development of Small Island Developing States and the outcome of the twenty-second special session of the General Assembly)
Target 15. Deal comprehensively with the debt problems of developing countries through national and international measures in order to make debt sustainable in the long term
[Some of the indicators listed below are monitored separately for the least developed countries (LDCs), Africa, landlocked countries and small island developing States]
Indicators
Official Development Assistance (ODA)
33. Net ODA, total and to LDCs, as percentage of OECD/DAC donors' gross national income (OECD)
34. Proportion of total bilateral, sector-allocable ODA of OECD/DAC donors to basic social services (basic education, primary health care, nutrition, safe water and sanitation) (OECD)
35. Proportion of bilateral ODA of OECD/DAC donors that is untied (OECD)
36. ODA received in landlocked countries as proportion of their GNIs (OECD)
37. ODA received in small island developing States as proportion of their GNIs (OECD)
Market Access
38. Proportion of total developed country imports (by value and excluding arms) from developing countries and from LDCs, admitted free of duties (UNCTAD) (not yet available)
39. Average tariffs imposed by developed countries on agricultural products and textiles and clothing from developing countries (UNCTAD) (not yet available)
40. Agricultural support estimate for OECD countries as percentage of their GDP (OECD)
41. Proportion of ODA provided to help build trade capacity (OECD, WTO) (not yet available)
Debt Sustainability
42. Total number of countries that have reached their HIPC decision points and number that have reached their HIPC completion points (cumulative) (IMF, World Bank) (see indicator 43 below)
43. Debt relief committed under HIPC initiative, US$ (IMF, World Bank)
44. Debt service as a percentage of exports of goods and services (IMF, World Bank)
Target 16. In cooperation with developing countries, develop and implement strategies for decent and productive work for youth
Indicator
45. Unemployment rate of 15- to 24-year-olds, each sex and total (ILO)
Target 17. In cooperation with pharmaceutical companies, provide access to affordable essential drugs in developing countries
Indicator
46. Proportion of population with access to affordable essential drugs on a sustainable basis (WHO)
Target 18. In cooperation with the private sector, make available the benefits of new technologies, especially information and communications
Indicators
47. Telephone lines and cellular subscribers per 100 population (ITU)
48. Personal computers in use per 100 population (ITU) and Internet users per 100 population (ITU)

* Agencies and organizations listed in parentheses provided the data to the MDG database.

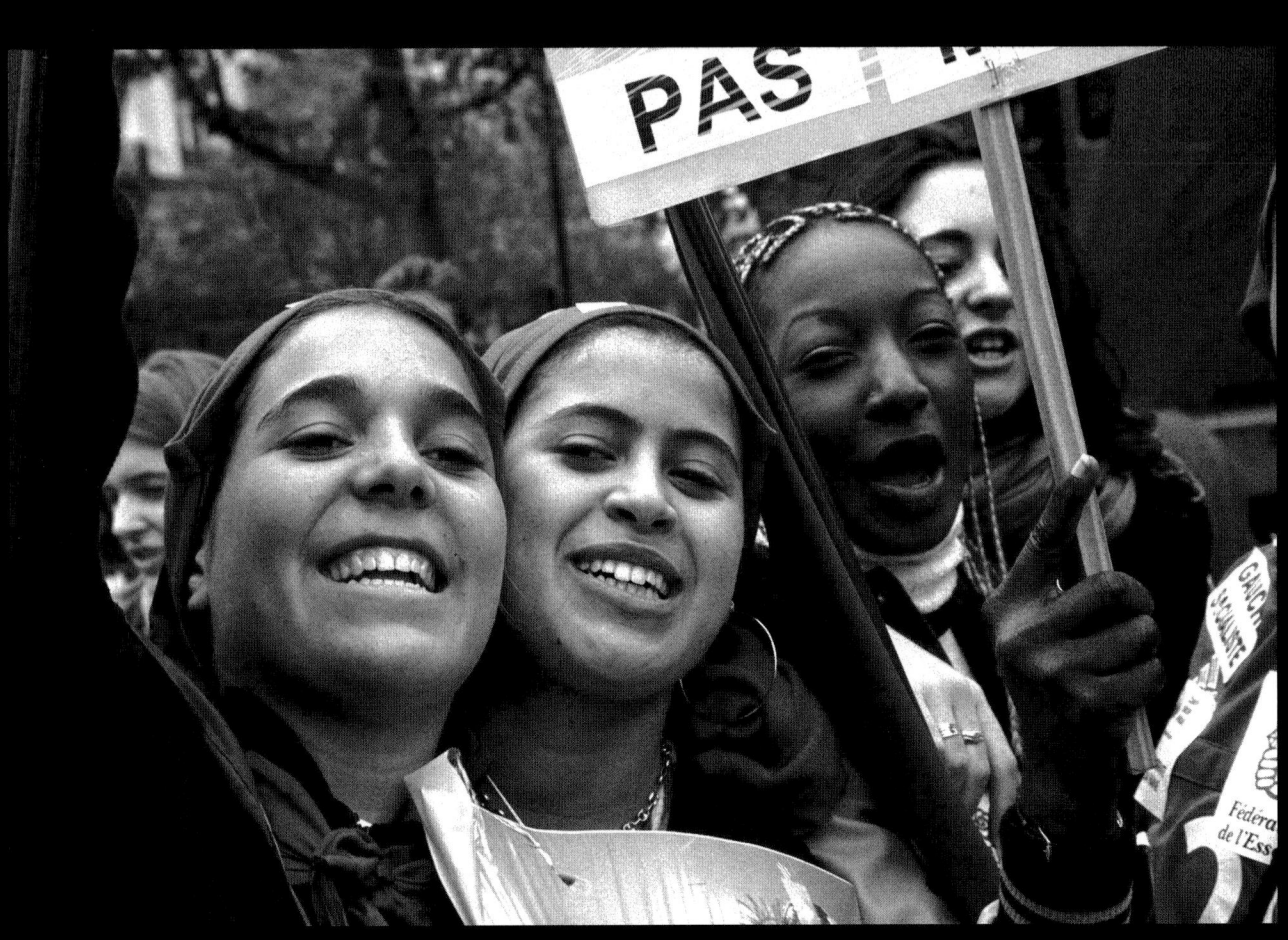
Young women at a political demonstration in Paris.

SECTION I

GENDER EQUALITY AND THE MILLENNIUM DEVELOPMENT GOALS

assessing progress in achieving gender equality

In this report we are presenting data for all four indicators relating to Goal 3 of the MDGs, since all four are necessary to fully show progress, or lack of it, in achieving the goal. The information provided here can be used to help women see where their own country is positioned, and give them the tools to push it forward. We have included data for all regions of the world (as classified by the UN system), including Western Europe and Other Developed Countries, because the promotion of gender equality and women's empowerment is a promise made to women throughout the world. It has never been an issue solely for developing countries. Like all indicators these four have their strengths and weaknesses. In particular, they are better interpreted as indicators of the extent to which some of the barriers to women's empowerment are crumbling, rather than as positive indicators of women's well-being. By tracking the indicators we can see, for instance, that in just two years women's enrolment in school has grown in some countries, and their literacy rates have increased, both of which are essential for women to participate as full citizens in their communities. Elsewhere, women have made dramatic gains in parliamentary elections and have taken on new powers of public decision-making. But the indicators don't tell us all we need to know about the efforts to improve women's lives. This is true for several reasons:

• *The indicators, like the target, are limited in scope.* They do not tell us about the terrible impact of violence against women on their lives. They do not tell us about the emotional toll of gender inequality and its effect on every aspect of women's lives. They do not tell us about the long, exhausting hours that women spend caring for their families and communities.

• *There is a tendency to use only the indicators relating to education* since the target for Goal 3 refers to schooling. This gives a misleading picture of women's empowerment. The *Human Development Report 2002* (UNDP), for example, provides a surprisingly optimistic picture of the achievements towards Goal 3. It shows no countries as 'lagging' (those that have achieved 70 to 89% of the rate of progress required to achieve the target by 2015) and only 13 as 'far behind' (those that have achieved less than 70% of the required rate of progress). In comparison, the goals for reducing hunger and infant and child mortality show many more countries either lagging or far behind — there are 59 countries far behind in achieving the goal for infant and child mortality, for example. But the only data presented for Goal 3 is for eliminating gender disparity in education enrolment. If the other indicators — literacy, wage employment and proportion of parliamentary seats — were included, the picture would be less rosy.

• *Ending disparity does not always equal empowerment.* Even

BOX 5: MILLENNIUM INDICATORS DATABASE

The United Nations Statistics Division (UNSD) has set up a millennium indicators site at www.millenniumindicators.un.org.

This site contains information about the 8 Millennium Development Goals, 18 targets and 48 indicators, as well as definitions and sources and background material on the adoption of the Millennium Declaration.

Information on the 48 indicators includes, to the extent it is available, background data for each of the world's countries or areas, which can be related to the MDG indicators. The data primarily covers the Millennium Declaration time frame for monitoring implementation — 1990-2015 — but earlier years are shown as reference points where available. Country profiles and world or regional trends can also be extracted from this page and specialised agencies such as UNESCO, WHO, ILO, UNAIDS, UNICEF, ITU, IPU, FAO, OECD, WB provide related statistics. It is possible to view, print or download all the data series.

By tracking the indicators we can see, for instance, that in just two years' time women's enrolment in school has grown in some countries, and their literacy rates have increased. These are both essential for women to participate as full citizens in their communities. Elsewhere, women have made dramatic gains in parliamentary elections and have taken on new powers of public decision-making.

when young women enter school in equal numbers with young men, they may still suffer harassment, or be discouraged from seeking higher education that might open up more jobs to them. Women may enter the workforce in the same numbers as men but still bump up against glass ceilings and unequal pay.

Nor does ending disparity guarantee that a majority of women or men are benefiting. Gender disparity would end if only 20 per cent of boys and girls attended school, but those low numbers would not empower anyone. In a report prepared by UNDP and UNICEF on the MDGs in Africa (UNDP/UNICEF 2002), the graphs on the ratio of girls' enrolment rates to boys' in primary education and on the ratio of literate females to males, aged 15 years and older show that disparity is slowly (too slowly) ending. However, even when there is no disparity and the gender gap in primary enrolment is closed, many young people will still not be in school. At the current rate, Africa will not meet Goal 2 of universal primary education until after the year 2100. Only seven African countries are on track to meet this goal by 2015.

PROGRESS IN THE CONTEXT OF THE MILLENNIUM DEVELOPMENT GOALS

To assess whether there have been improvements since *Progress of the World's Women 2000* was published, we look at recent changes. The data comes from compilations and estimations made by international organizations on the basis of information supplied by national governments. In some cases, two years is not enough time for significant change to show up, but we can see patterns that reveal causes for concern as well as optimism. The pattern varies by region, with the biggest deficits in education, literacy and non-agricultural wage employment tending to be in the poorest countries or those cultures with a strong preference for sons. Women's share of seats in parliament depends less on economic strength than on the political will of governments.

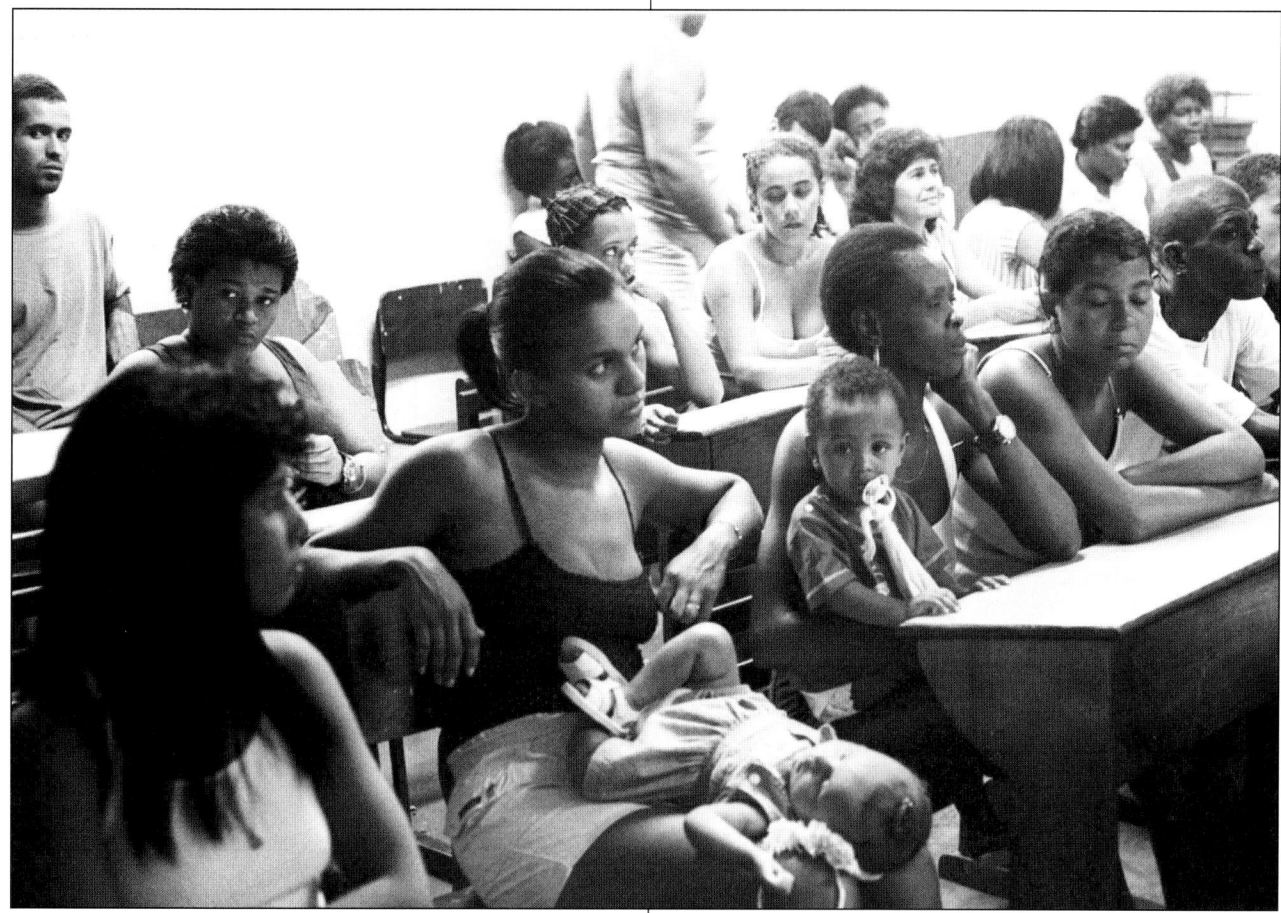

An adult education class in Rio de Janeiro.

Key Findings

• Only seven developed countries — Sweden, Denmark, Finland, Norway, Iceland, Netherlands and Germany — have achieved high levels of gender equality and women's empowerment on all the selected indicators.
• The developing countries with the highest levels of gender equality and women's empowerment on the selected indicators are Argentina, Costa Rica and South Africa.
• The greatest improvements have occurred in women's share of seats in parliament.
• The countries with the lowest achievement in education, literacy and non-agricultural wage employment tend to be the poorest. But women's share of seats in parliament is not related to wealth and is highest where special measures have been introduced to help get women elected, as in Mozambique where women now hold 30 per cent of the seats.
• Countries in which there is a strong cultural preference for sons also tend towards the lowest levels of gender equality.
• In many of the countries with the lowest scores, progress is too slow.

The same seven northern European countries that had the highest achievement in 2000 are the leaders again in 2002. South Africa was the leading developing country two years ago, and has now been joined by Argentina and Costa Rica as a result of large increases in women's share of seats in parliament in those two countries. Of course, this does not mean that all other dimensions of women's lives have improved: In Argentina, for instance, the recent financial crisis has thrown nearly everyone's life into disarray, leaving women especially hard hit. Their wages have decreased, their rates of unemployment have increased and their poverty has deepened.

In general, the most positive changes since the *Progress 2000* report are in women's share of seats in parliament because this can be changed quickly in a short space of time if there is the political will. Changes in literacy, education and employment are rarely so dramatic in a similarly short space of time, since they require widespread changes in economic and cultural structures.

It is clear that in the poorest countries, women will need the support of a more just international system to achieve gender equality and empowerment; the increase in international inequality will have to be reversed.

EDUCATION: SECONDARY SCHOOL ENROLMENT

Key Findings

- A majority of countries cited in this report have achieved gender equality in secondary school education or have more girls enrolled at the secondary level than boys.
- 2 per cent of the countries have achieved gender equality in educational enrolment at the secondary level.
- 48 per cent have a higher secondary school enrolment rate for girls than for boys, often because boys leave school for employment earlier than girls.
- 34 per cent, mainly in sub-Saharan Africa and South Asia, have a lower enrolment rate for girls than boys.
- For the remaining 16 per cent there is no up to date data available from UNESCO.

The Gender Gap in Secondary School Enrolment

We have chosen to focus on secondary level education because primary education is being tracked in relation to Goal 2. Without secondary education women are often excluded from better-paying jobs and positions of responsibility.

Chart 1 (p. 16) shows gender disparity in secondary schooling as measured by the ratio between girls' and boys' secondary net or gross enrolment rates.

- a score of 100 indicates that the two enrolment rates are equal
- below 100 means that girls' rate is lower than boys', the traditional definition of a gender gap
- above 100 means that boys have a lower enrolment rate, often called a reverse gender gap

The chart shows that girls' inequality is worst in sub-Saharan Africa, in which 31 countries have a gender gap, with the interlinked dynamics of poverty, HIV/AIDS and conflict as the major reasons. On the other hand, the significant gender gap in girls' enrolment in Asia and the Pacific occurs primarily in South Asia, where poverty plays a role but where there is also a strong preference for sons in many communities. Too often, daughters are considered a liability whose education would be a waste of time and money.

The reverse gender gap — with a higher rate for girls' enrolment than for boys' — is more prevalent in the other regions of the world, including Northern Africa, Central and Western Asia and Latin America and the Caribbean. In the last region, 20 countries have a reverse gender gap and only three

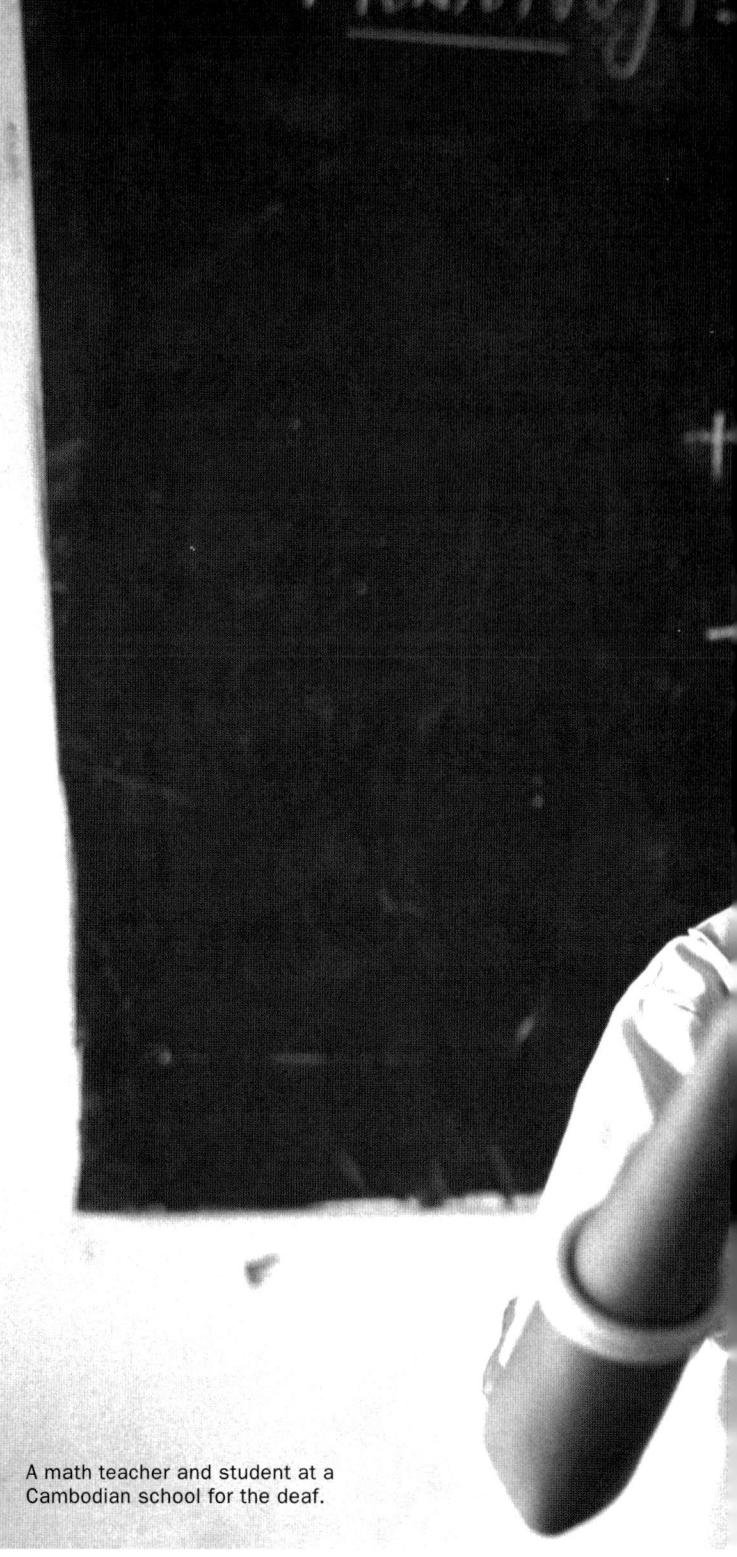

A math teacher and student at a Cambodian school for the deaf.

a gender gap. The reverse gender gap is also common in developed countries, where 19 have a reverse gap, four have a gender gap and only one has an equal ratio of girls and boys in school.

Although nearly half the countries surveyed had a higher enrolment rate for girls than boys, this does not mean that girls in those countries are more empowered than boys. Nor do the gender gaps in education match the gender gaps in adult life: In countries that have a higher enrolment for girls than boys, men are still likely to earn more than women when they enter the job market. This is because gender discrimination pervades the labour market in most countries and because women spend more time providing the unpaid care work that

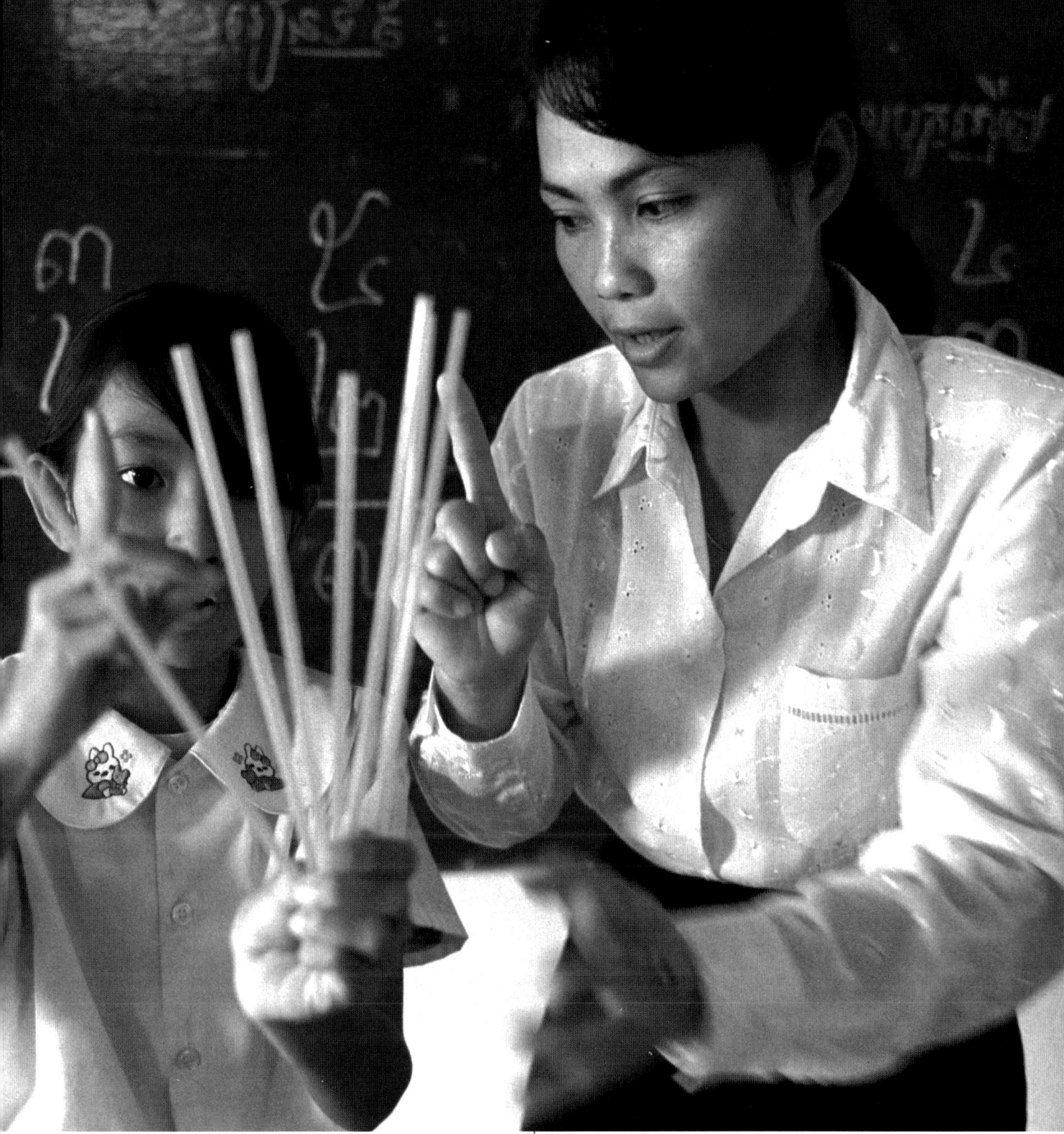

PHOTO BY JOHN VINK-MAGNUM PHOTOS

supports their families than men do.

In addition, some of the highest reverse gender gap scores are in countries where girls' enrolment is still very low. For example, Lesotho has a reverse gender gap score of 161 but girls' net enrolment rate is only 24 per cent, and boys' rate, of course, is even lower.

The *level* of girls' enrolment in secondary school is a better signpost of women's empowerment because it can show whether equality has been achieved at a high level of enrolment or a low one. Our research shows that only 20 countries have 90 per cent or more of secondary school-age girls enrolled in school, and most of these countries are in Western Europe and Other Developed Countries. To ensure that more girls, many of whom are poor and cannot afford school fees, are enrolled, the focus for action must be on providing the means to get them into secondary education, rather than on simply ending gender disparities in enrolment.

Table 1 (p. 18-19) shows girls' secondary enrolment rate. It indicates that for many countries there is still a long way to go to achieve full enrolment. It will be important to keep track of these numbers in order to guide policy. It would be even better to begin to track completion rates, which would give a clearer picture of girls' ability to compete in the job market.

CHART 1: Secondary Level Enrolment, Ratio of Female Rate to Male Rate, 1999/2000

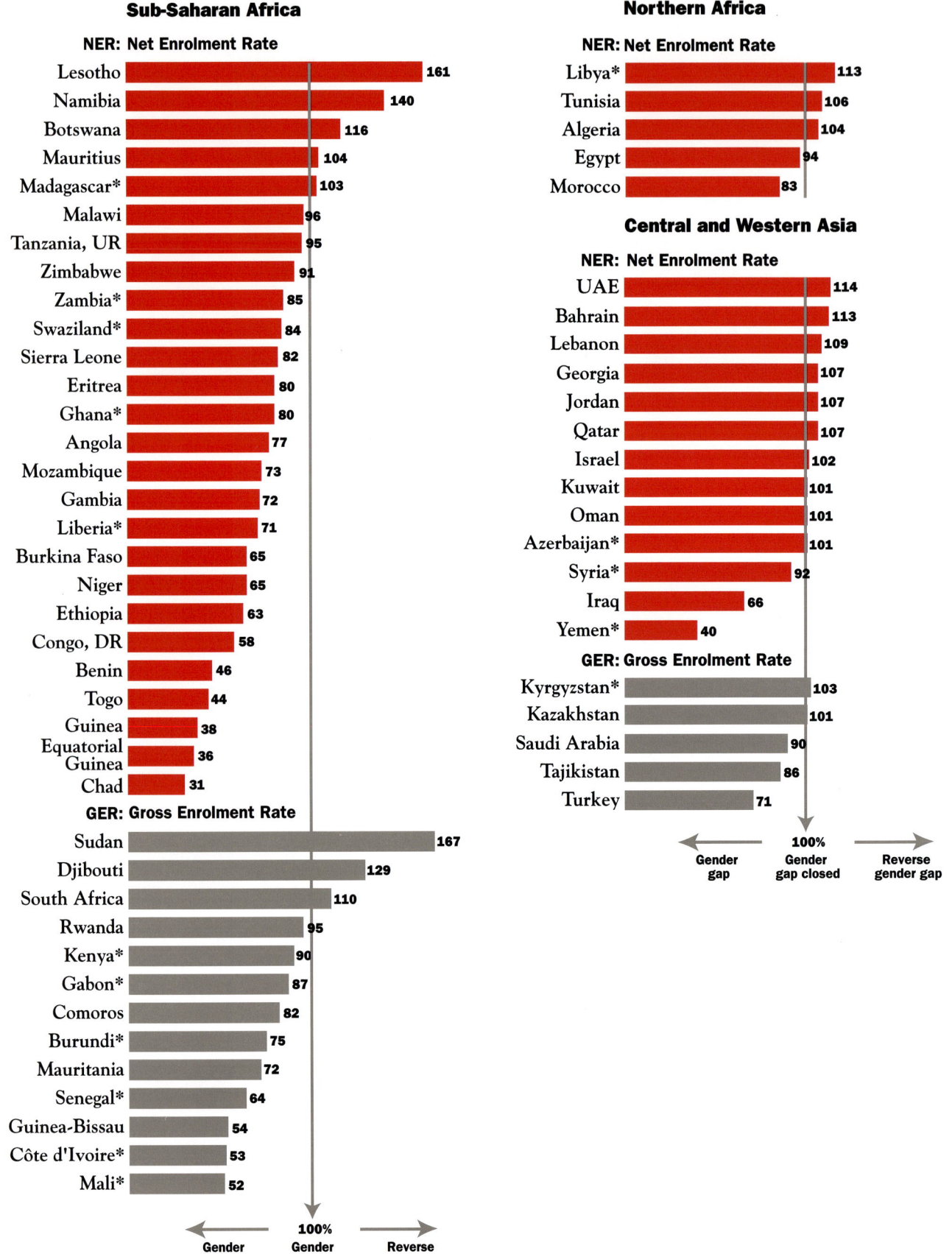

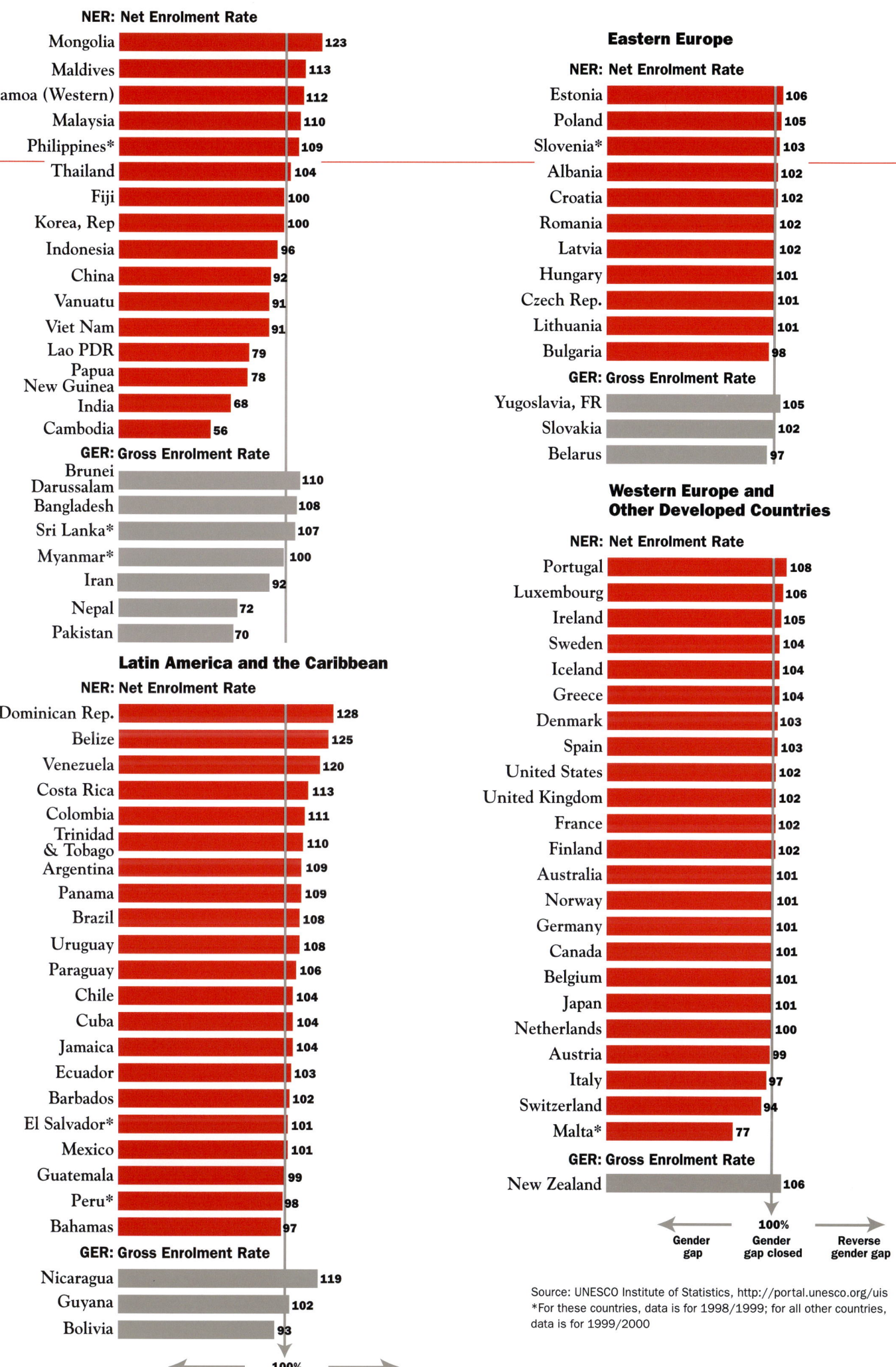

Table 1: Female Enrolment in Secondary Education, 1999/2000

SUB-SAHARAN AFRICA

	Net Rate
Mauritius	74
Botswana	63
Namibia	40
Malawi	40
Zimbabwe	40
Swaziland*	35
Ghana	23
Lesotho	24
Sierra Leone	22
Gambia	20
Eritrea	20
Zambia*	19
Liberia	17
Togo	14
Equatorial Guinea	14
Ethiopia	12
Madagascar	12
Benin	11
Congo, DR	9
Guinea	7
Burkina Faso	7
Niger	5
Mozambique	6
Tanzania, UR	5
Chad	4
	Gross Rate
South Africa	95
Gabon*	51
Sudan	36
Kenya*	28
Comoros	19
Djibouti	17
Senegal*	15
Mauritania	15
Côte d'Ivoire*	15
Guinea-Bissau	14
Angola	13
Rwanda	12
Mali*	10
Burundi*	6
Cameroon	n.d
Cape Verde	n.d
Central African Rep.	n.d
Congo	n.d
Nigeria	n.d
Reunion	n.d
Seychelles	n.d
Somalia	n.d
Uganda	n.d

NORTHERN AFRICA

	Net Rate
Egypt	77
Libya*	76
Tunisia	70
Algeria	60
Morocco	27

CENTRAL AND WESTERN ASIA

	Net Rate
Israel	89
Bahrain	87
Qatar	82
Azerbaijan*	78
Jordan	78
Lebanon	73
UAE	72
Oman	59
Georgia	56
Kuwait	50
Syria*	36
Iraq	26
Yemen*	21
	Gross Rate
Kazakhstan	87
Kyrgyzstan	84
Tajikistan	67
Saudi Arabia	65
Turkey	46
Armenia	n.d
Cyprus	n.d
Turkmenistan	n.d
Uzbekistan	n.d

ASIA AND THE PACIFIC

	Net Rate
Korea, Rep.	94
Malaysia	93
Fiji	76
Samoa (Western)	73
Mongolia	65
Viet Nam	58
Thailand	57
Philippines*	53
China	48
Indonesia	46
Maldives	33
India	31
Vanuatu	21
Lao PDR	25
Papua New Guinea	18
Cambodia	11
	Gross Rate
Brunei Darussalam	116
Iran	77
Sri Lanka*	74
Bangladesh	56
Nepal	45
Myanmar*	35
Pakistan	32
Afghanistan	n.d
East Timor, DR	n.d
Hong Kong, China	n.d
Korea, DPR	n.d
Singapore	n.d

LATIN AMERICA AND THE CARIBBEAN

	Net Rate
Uruguay	81
Cuba	81
Argentina	79
Jamaica	76
Chile	73
Barbados	71
Brazil	71
Trinidad & Tobago	67
Panama	64
Peru*	61
Mexico	58
Colombia	57
Venezuela	55
Ecuador	48
Costa Rica	46
Paraguay	46
Dominican Rep.	45
Belize	40
El Salvador*	38
Guatemala	18
	Gross Rate
Guyana*	82
Bolivia	76
Nicaragua	65
Bahamas	n.d
Haiti	n.d
Honduras	n.d
Suriname	n.d

EASTERN EUROPE

	Net Rate
Estonia	93
Slovenia*	91
Hungary	88
Lithuania	88
Latvia	85
Czech Rep.	85
Bulgaria	85
Croatia	80
Romania	77
Poland	77
Albania	73
	Gross Rate
Belarus	93
Slovakia	87
Yugoslavia, FR	62
Bosnia-Herzegovina	n.d
Macedonia, FYR	n.d
Moldova, Rep.	n.d
Russian Fed.	n.d
Ukraine	n.d

WESTERN EUROPE AND OTHER DEVELOPED COUNTRIES

	Net Rate
Ireland	100
Japan	100
Sweden	98
Canada	98
Norway	96
Finland	96
Belgium	96
United Kingdom	95
France	94
Netherlands	92
Spain	92
Portugal	91
Denmark	91
Austria	89
Australia	88
United States	88
Greece	88
Germany	88
Switzerland	86
Italy	86
Luxembourg	85
Iceland	78
Malta	77
	Gross Rate
New Zealand	116

Sources: UNESCO Institute of Statistics, http://portal.unesco.org/uis
* For these countries, data is for 1998/1999; for all other countries data is for 1999/2000

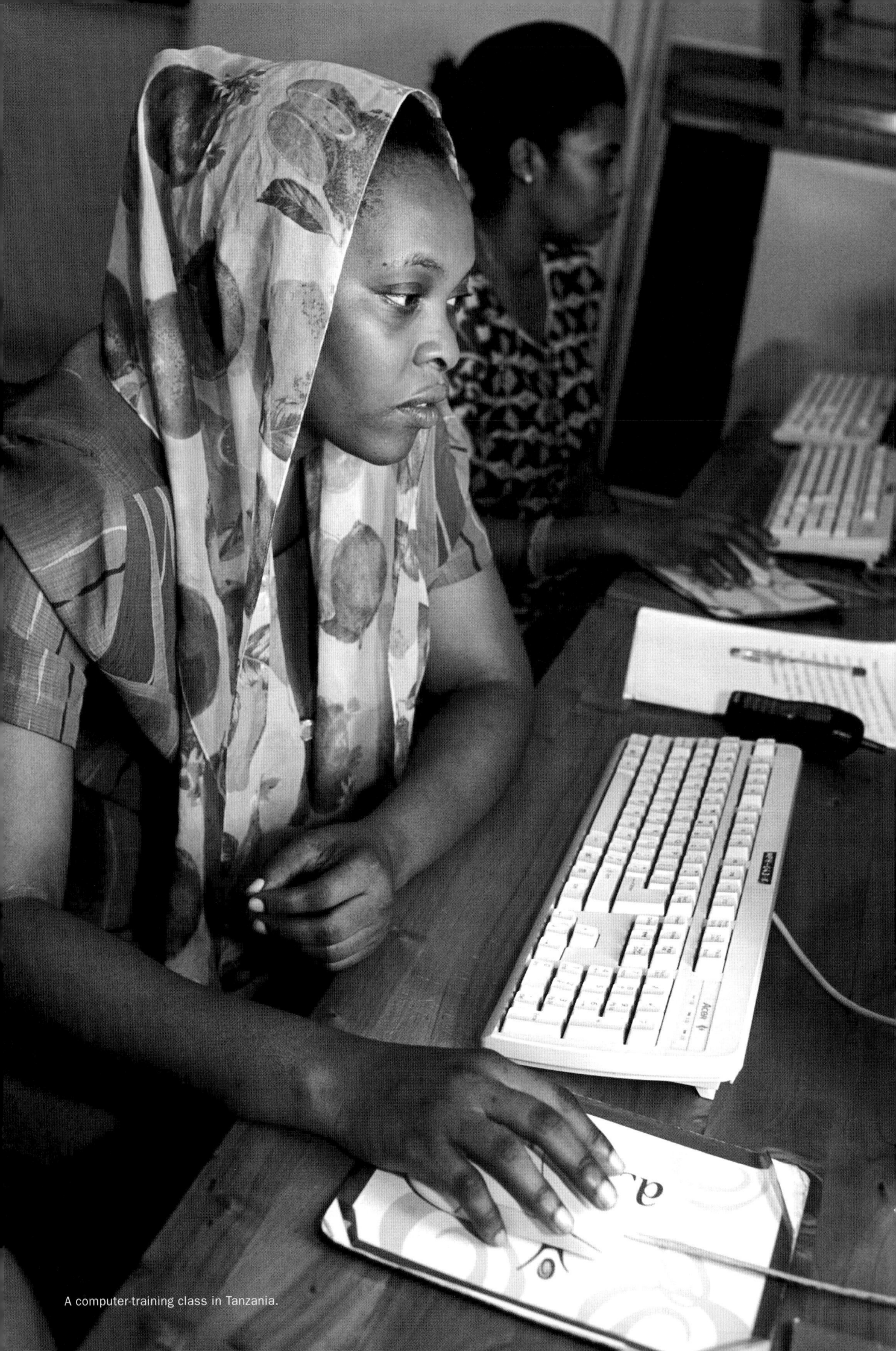
A computer-training class in Tanzania.

LITERACY

Key Findings

• There are an estimated 140 million illiterate young people in the world, of whom more than half — 86 million — are young women.
• 34 per cent of the countries covered in this report have achieved gender equality in youth literacy rates.
• 38 per cent, mainly in sub-Saharan Africa and South Asia, have a lower literacy rate for girls than boys.
• 14 per cent have a lower literacy rate for boys than girls.
• For the remaining 14 per cent there is no data available from UNESCO.
• In the period between 1995 and 2002, there were improvements in the literacy of young women in all the countries where there was still room for improvement.
• In those countries where less than 50 per cent of young women are literate, progress has been too slow. At current rates, none of these countries will achieve literacy for all young women by 2015.
• If current rates continue, UNESCO projects that in 2015 there will be an estimated 107 million illiterate young people, and again more than half — 67 million — will be young women.

The Gender Gap in Literacy

The literacy rate is in some ways a stronger indicator of young women's empowerment than education. It shows whether young women's schooling has equipped them with the ability to communicate by reading and writing, a set of critical skills for earning a living and participating in public decision-making.

The MDG literacy indicator is measured by the ratio of the female youth literacy rate to the male youth literacy rate. This indicator is shown in Chart 2 using data compiled by UNESCO for the MDG database. Questions have been raised about the quality of the data because most countries rely on proxy measures to gauge literacy, such as years of schooling, rather than actual tests. However, there is no alternative data available at the moment. Chart 2 (pp. 22-23) is organized in the same way as the chart for gender disparity in secondary education enrolment: A score of 100 means the rates are equal; below 100 means that the female youth literacy rate is lower than the male one (creating a gender gap); and a score above 100 means the male youth literacy rate is lower than the female (creating a reverse gender gap).

The data suggests that there is much more of a gender gap in literacy rates than there was in school enrolment. The problem is greatest in sub-Saharan Africa where 35 out of 41 countries have a ratio of less than 100 literate females for every 100 literate males. There are particularly large gaps in parts of West Africa, where the lowest ratio is 44 in Niger. In comparison, in Northern Africa, where all four countries have a gender gap ratio of less than 100, the lowest is only 79 (Morocco).

As with school enrolment, the main problem in Asia is in South Asia, especially in Bangladesh, Nepal and Pakistan. In Latin America and the Caribbean, most countries are at or near equality in literacy rates, and Eastern Europe has achieved gender equality in youth literacy with the sole exception of Albania, which is nevertheless close to equality. The ratio is not below 100 in any of the nations of Western Europe and Other Developed countries.

Again, as was the case when comparing enrolment rates, ending gender disparity is still an important objective in sub-Saharan Africa and South Asia where women's rates of literacy are much lower than men's.

As with secondary school enrolment, while many — 34 per cent — of the countries in this report have achieved gender equality in youth literacy rates, this indicator does not tell us the actual levels of young women's literacy, which would be a better indicator of achievement.

Table 2 shows the actual literacy rate of young women in 2002 by region. Not surprisingly, 95 per cent or more of young women are literate in Western Europe and Other Developed Countries. In the rest of the world, 95 per cent or more of young women are literate in 61 countries; between 50 per cent and 95 per cent are literate in 54 countries; and less than 50 per cent are literate in 11 countries.

In Central and Western Asia more than half (10 out of 17) of the nations for which there is data have achieved almost full literacy for women. In Asia and the Pacific nearly half (15 out of 24 countries for which there is data) have almost full literacy. Illiteracy remains an acute problem in both sub-Saharan Africa and South Asia.

Changes in Female Youth Literacy Rate

Chart 3 (pp. 26-29) maps the changes in female youth literacy from 1995 to 2002. It is encouraging to note that no countries have slipped from their 1995 position, and some of the biggest increases have been in countries which previously had the lowest levels of female youth literacy: Burkina Faso, Guinea Bissau, Mali, Niger and Yemen. But the rate of increase in countries with low levels of literacy is still too slow, as is evident in Table 3 (p. 29), which shows how long it will take the countries with the lowest levels of female youth literacy to achieve rates of 95 per cent or above.

CHART 2: Ratio of Female Youth Literacy Rate to Male Youth Literacy Rate, 2002

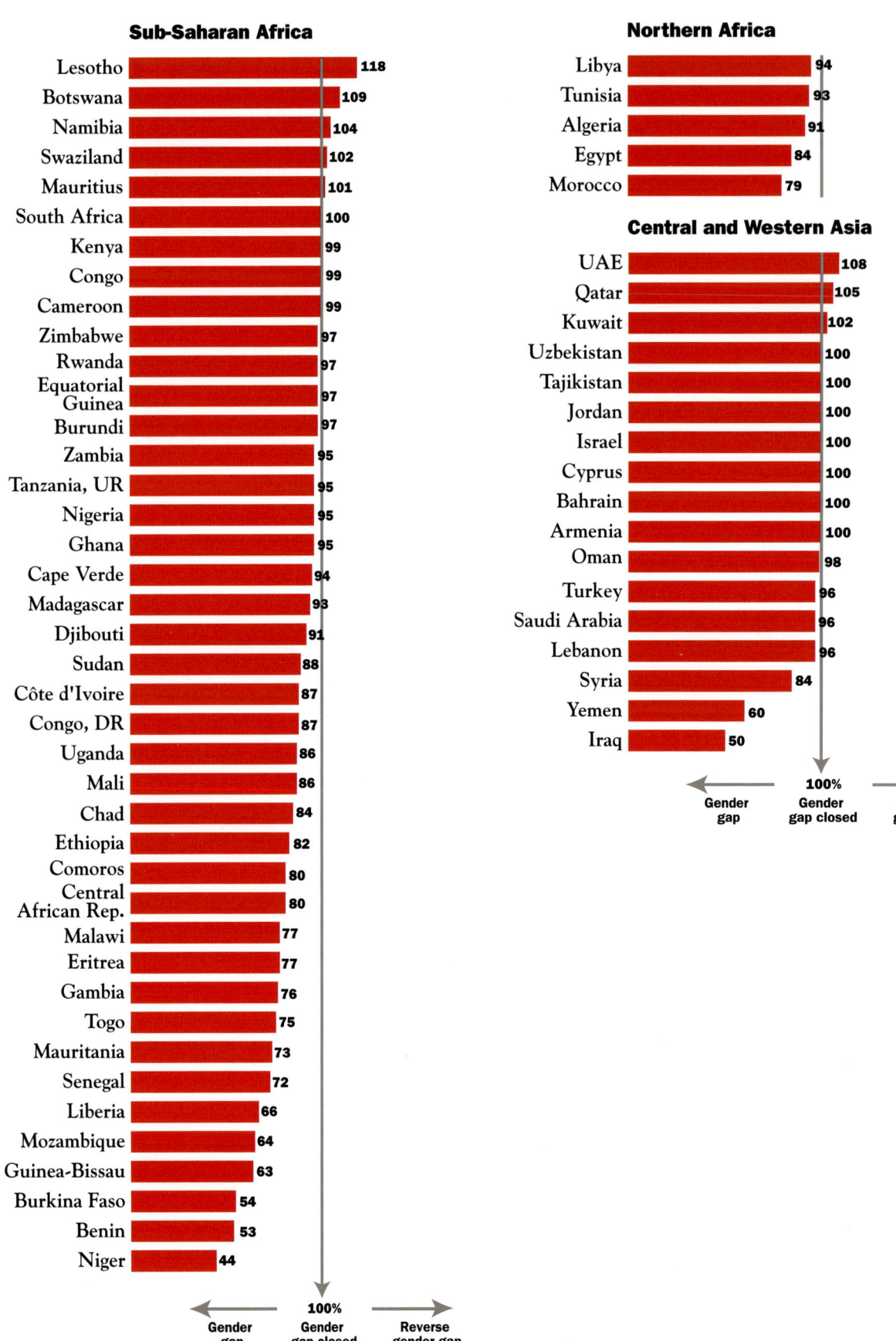

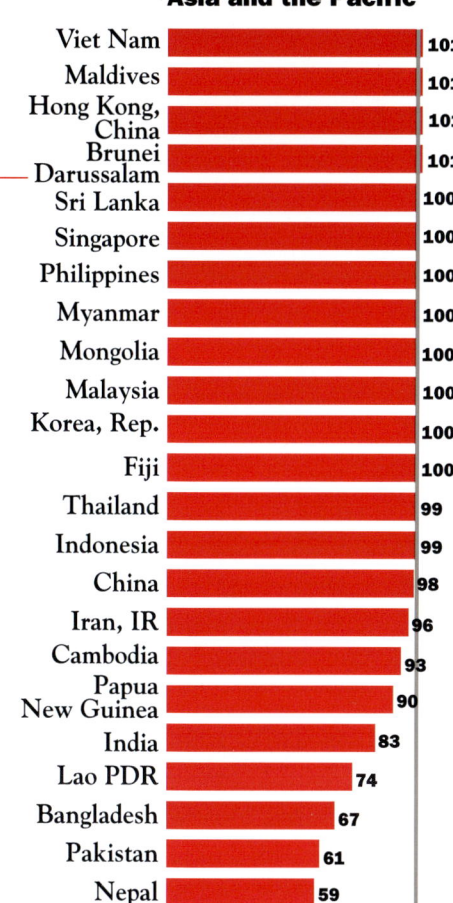
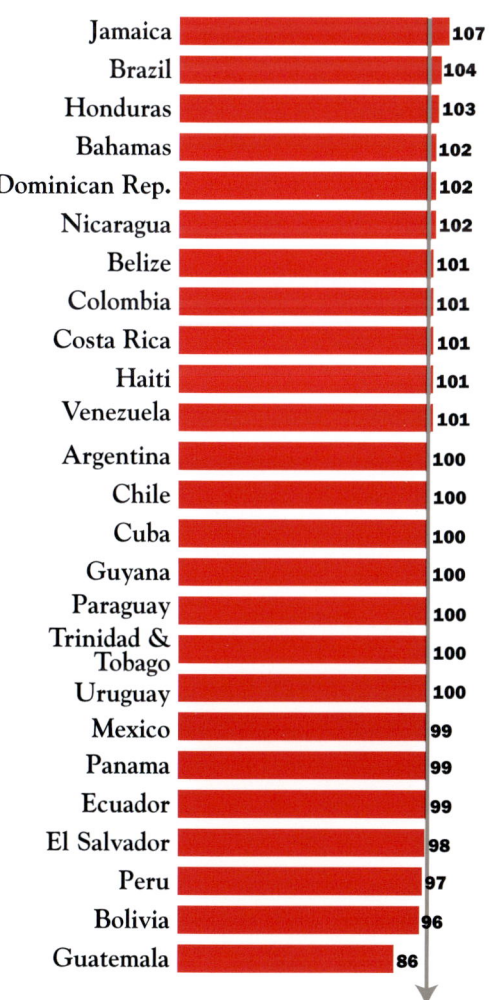
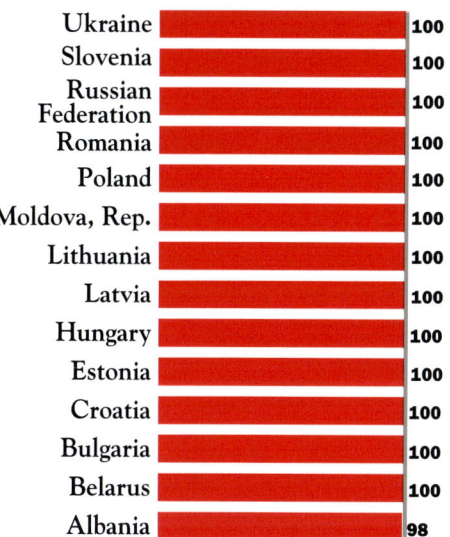
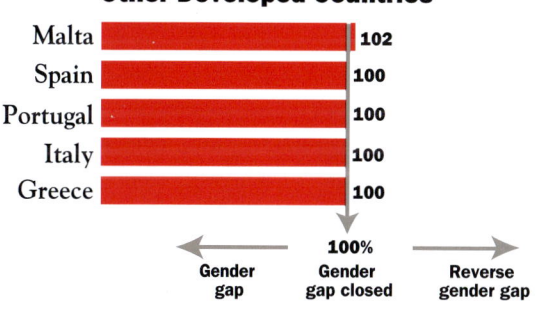

Source: Millennium Indicators Database, http://millenniumindicators.un.org

Table 2: Female Youth (ages 15-24) Literacy Rate (%), 2002

SUB-SAHARAN AFRICA

Lesotho	98.7
Congo	97.3
Zimbabwe	96.3
Eq. Guinea	96.1
Kenya	95.1
Mauritius	94.9
Namibia	94.0
Cameroon	93.9
Botswana	92.8
Swaziland	92.1
South Africa	91.7
Ghana	89.9
Tanzania, UR	89.4
Zambia	86.8
Cape Verde	86.4
Nigeria	86.1
Rwanda	83.4
Djibouti	81.7
Madagascar	78.3
Congo, DR	77.7
Uganda	74.1
Sudan	74.1
Togo	66.5
Burundi	65.1
Mali	64.5
Chad	64.0
Côte d'Ivoire	63.1
Malawi	62.8
Eritrea	62.5
Central African Republic	62.4
Liberia	57.2
Comoros	52.3
Gambia	51.9
Ethiopia	51.4
Mozambique	49.2
Guinea-Bissau	47.1
Senegal	44.3
Mauritania	41.8
Benin	38.5
Burkina Faso	25.7
Niger	14.9
Angola	n.d
Gabon	n.d
Guinea	n.d
Reunion	n.d
Seychelles	n.d
Sierra Leone	n.d
Somalia	n.d

NORTHERN AFRICA

Libya	94.1
Tunisia	90.6
Algeria	86.3
Egypt	64.8
Morocco	61.4

CENTRAL AND WESTERN ASIA

Cyprus	99.8
Tajikistan	99.8
Armenia	99.7
Uzbekistan	99.6
Jordan	99.5
Israel	99.3
Bahrain	98.8
Qatar	97.5
Oman	97.4
UAE	95.1
Turkey	94.8
Kuwait	93.9
Lebanon	93.7
Saudi Arabia	91.6
Syria	80.6
Yemen	50.5
Iraq	29.9
Azerbaijan	n.d
Georgia	n.d
Kazakhstan	n.d
Kyrgyzstan	n.d
Turkmenistan	n.d

ASIA AND THE PACIFIC

Brunei Darussalam	99.8
Hong Kong, China	99.8
Korea, Rep.	99.8
Mongolia	99.8
Samoa (Western)	99.8
Singapore	99.8
Maldives	99.5
Fiji	99.2
China	99.2
Philippines	99.0
Thailand	98.5
Malaysia	98.0
Indonesia	97.6
Viet Nam	97.5
Sri Lanka	96.9
Iran, IR	92.7
Myanmar	91.1
Cambodia	77.0
Papua New Guinea	72.9
India	66.8
Lao PDR	62.3
Nepal	46.0
Pakistan	44.2
Bangladesh	41.4
Afghanistan	n.d
East Timor, DR	n.d
Korea, DPR	n.d
Vanuatu	n.d

LATIN AMERICA AND THE CARIBBEAN	
Cuba	99.8
Guyana	99.8
Trinidad & Tobago	99.8
Uruguay	99.6
Chile	99.2
Argentina	98.9
Belize	98.9
Venezuela	98.9
Costa Rica	98.7
Bahamas	98.4
Colombia	97.9
Jamaica	97.8
Paraguay	97.3
Ecuador	97.3
Mexico	96.9
Panama	96.6
Peru	95.8
Brazil	94.8
Bolivia	94.4
Dominican Rep.	92.4
El Salvador	88.2
Honduras	85.5
Guatemala	74.0
Nicaragua	73.0
Haiti	66.5
Barbados	n.d
Suriname	n.d

EASTERN EUROPE	
Ukraine	99.9
Belarus	99.8
Croatia	99.8
Estonia	99.8
Hungary	99.8
Latvia	99.8
Lithuania	99.8
Moldova, Rep.	99.8
Poland	99.8
Russian Federation	99.8
Slovenia	99.8
Romania	99.7
Bulgaria	99.6
Albania	96.9
Bosnia-Herzegovina	n.d
Czech Republic	n.d
Macedonia, FYR	n.d
Slovakia	n.d
Yugoslavia	n.d

WESTERN EUROPE AND OTHER DEVELOPED COUNTRIES	
Greece	99.8
Italy	99.8
Malta	99.8
Portugal	99.8
Spain	99.8

Source: Millennium Indicators Database
http://millenniumindicators.un.org

CHART 3: Changes in Female Youth Literacy Rate,

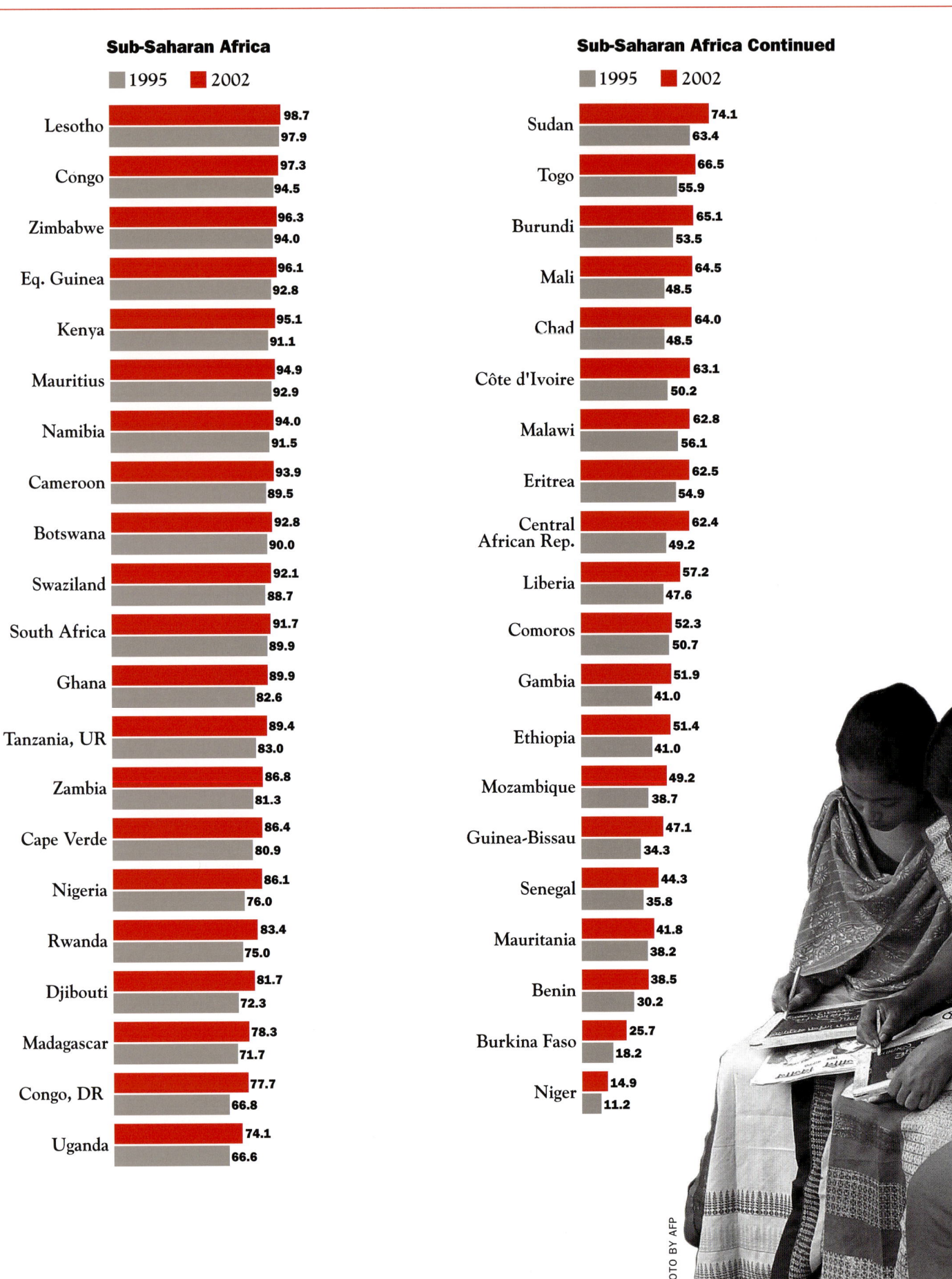

Sub-Saharan Africa

■ 1995 ■ 2002

Country	1995	2002
Lesotho	97.9	98.7
Congo	94.5	97.3
Zimbabwe	94.0	96.3
Eq. Guinea	92.8	96.1
Kenya	91.1	95.1
Mauritius	92.9	94.9
Namibia	91.5	94.0
Cameroon	89.5	93.9
Botswana	90.0	92.8
Swaziland	88.7	92.1
South Africa	89.9	91.7
Ghana	82.6	89.9
Tanzania, UR	83.0	89.4
Zambia	81.3	86.8
Cape Verde	80.9	86.4
Nigeria	76.0	86.1
Rwanda	75.0	83.4
Djibouti	72.3	81.7
Madagascar	71.7	78.3
Congo, DR	66.8	77.7
Uganda	66.6	74.1

Sub-Saharan Africa Continued

■ 1995 ■ 2002

Country	1995	2002
Sudan	63.4	74.1
Togo	55.9	66.5
Burundi	53.5	65.1
Mali	48.5	64.5
Chad	48.5	64.0
Côte d'Ivoire	50.2	63.1
Malawi	56.1	62.8
Eritrea	54.9	62.5
Central African Rep.	49.2	62.4
Liberia	47.6	57.2
Comoros	50.7	52.3
Gambia	41.0	51.9
Ethiopia	41.0	51.4
Mozambique	38.7	49.2
Guinea-Bissau	34.3	47.1
Senegal	35.8	44.3
Mauritania	38.2	41.8
Benin	30.2	38.5
Burkina Faso	18.2	25.7
Niger	11.2	14.9

PHOTO BY AFP

26 • ASSESSING PROGRESS

1995-2002

Northern Africa
■ 1995 ■ 2002

Country	2002	1995
Libya	94.1	88.9
Tunisia	90.6	83.7
Algeria	86.3	77.2
Egypt	64.8	57.0
Morocco	61.4	40.1

Central and Western Asia
■ 1995 ■ 2002

Country	2002	1995
Tajikistan	99.8	99.8
Cyprus	99.8	99.8
Armenia	99.7	99.6
Uzbekistan	99.6	99.6
Jordan	99.5	97.9
Israel	99.3	98.8
Bahrain	98.8	97.3
Qatar	97.5	95.5
Oman	97.4	89.6
UAE	95.1	92.0
Turkey	94.8	91.6
Kuwait	93.9	90.8
Lebanon	93.7	91.0
Saudi Arabia	91.6	85.6
Syria	80.6	73.3
Yemen	50.5	35.0
Iraq	29.9	26.9

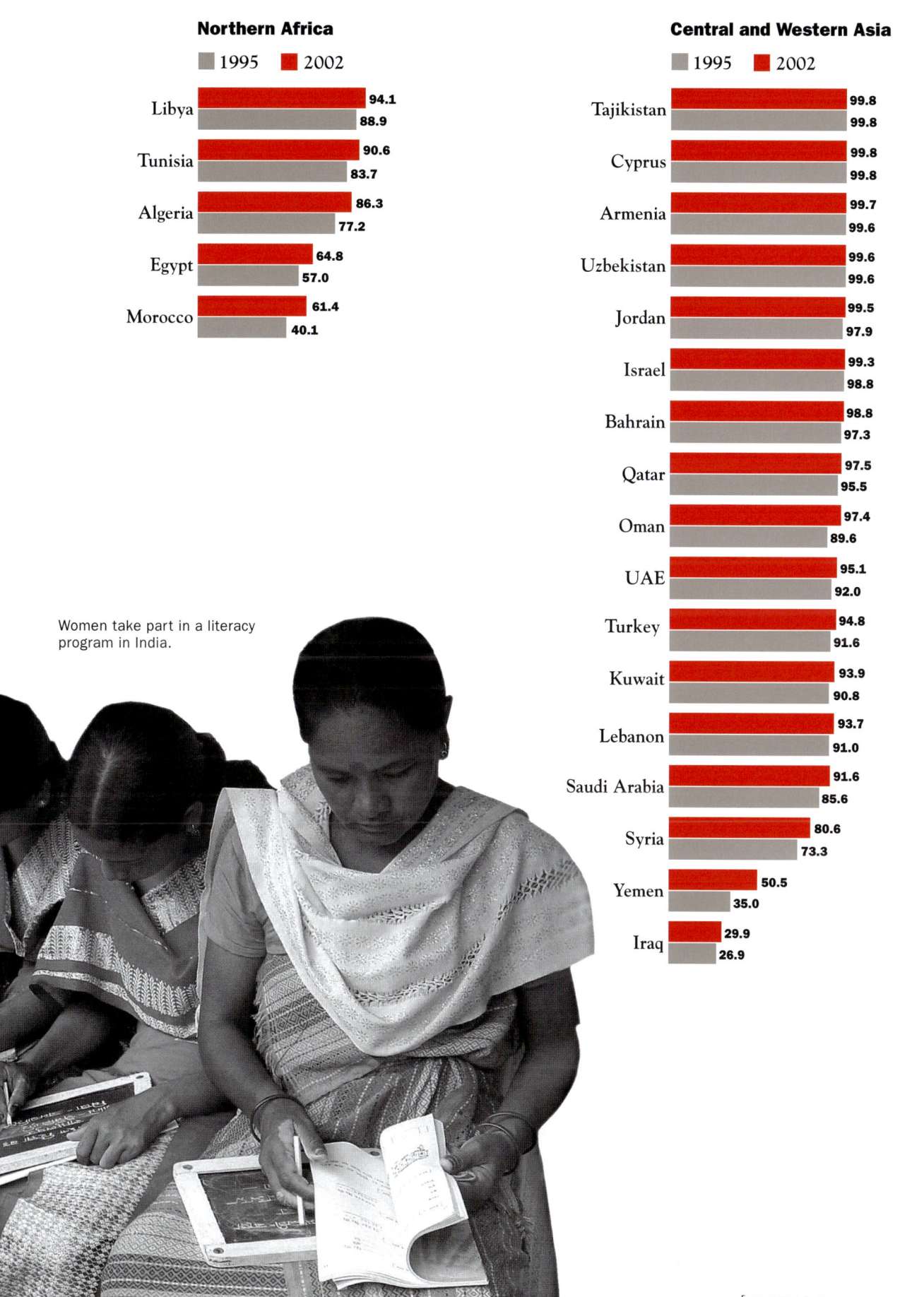

Women take part in a literacy program in India.

[CHART CONTINUED ON PAGE 28]

CHART 3: Changes in Female Youth Literacy Rate, 1995-2002 (cont'd.)

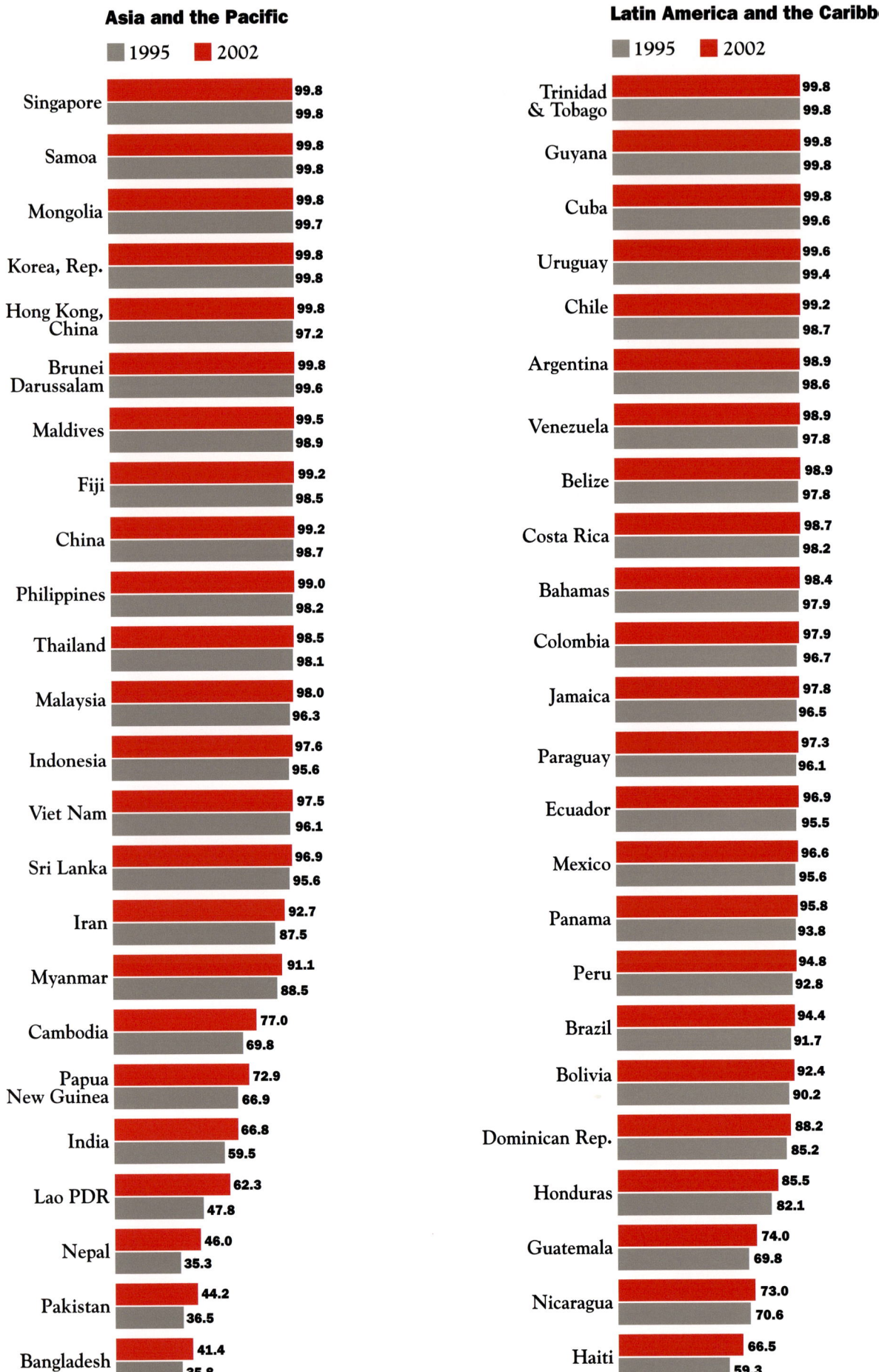

Eastern Europe

■ 1995 ■ 2002

Country	2002	1995
Ukraine	99.9	99.9
Slovenia	99.8	99.8
Russian Federation	99.8	99.8
Poland	99.8	99.8
Moldova, Rep.	99.8	99.8
Lithuania	99.8	99.8
Latvia	99.8	99.8
Hungary	99.8	99.8
Estonia	99.8	99.8
Croatia	99.8	99.7
Belarus	99.8	99.8
Romania	99.7	99.5
Bulgaria	99.6	99.4
Albania	96.9	94.6

Western Europe and Other Developed Countries

■ 1995 ■ 2002

Country	2002	1995
Greece	99.8	99.8
Italy	99.8	99.8
Malta	99.8	99.6
Portugal	99.8	99.8
Spain	99.8	99.8

Source: Millennium Indicators Database
http://millenniumindicators.un.org

Table 3: Length of Time Needed to Achieve 95% Female Youth Literacy Rate at Current Rates of Change

	Female Youth Literacy Rate (%) 2002	Average Annual Rate of Change (%) 1988-2002	Number of Years Needed to Reach 95%
Iraq	29.9	1.6	74
Niger	14.9	4.1	45
Bangladesh	41.4	2.1	40
Mauritania	41.8	2.1	38
Burkina Faso	25.7	5.2	25
Pakistan	44.2	3.2	24
Benin	35.8	3.8	23
Senegal	44.3	3.3	23
Mozambique	49.2	3.8	17
Nepal	46.0	4.8	15
Guinea-Bissau	47.4	5.0	14

EMPLOYMENT

Key Findings

• Women's share of non-agricultural wage employment approaches parity with that of men (is in the range of 45-55%) in less than half the countries (39 out of 87) for which data is available.
• Some evidence suggests that gender gaps persist in pay and conditions even when women's share of jobs approaches parity with men's share.
• Trends in women's share of wage employment in non-agricultural employment from the mid 1980s are mixed. Although women's share is increasing in most countries and barriers to their employment in industry and services are clearly crumbling, the benefits to women are less clear.
• The poorest women in the world are employed in agriculture or 'informal' manufacturing and services and their work is vastly undercounted in employment statistics. Indicators and targets that track employment in these areas need to be set up and monitored at the national level.

The Gender Gap in Non-Agricultural Wage Employment

As globalization has spread, moving manufacturing jobs from the developed to the developing world, women's share of non-agricultural wage employment has increased. But women remain in primarily sex-segregated jobs with lower pay and less job security. They are also suffering disproportionately from the slowdown in the global economy, which has forced many into informal, precarious work with few rights or benefits. And even as they take on more responsibilities in the paid employment sector, they remain the primary caretakers of their families. Very little of this is evident in the indicator chosen to track the realization of Goal 3 in the economy: the share of women in wage employment in the non-agricultural sector. Thus, as with the other indicators, this should not be seen as an indicator of women's well being, but of the extent to which women have equal access to this type of employment.

Table 4 (pp. 32-33) shows the female share of wage employment in the non-agricultural sector, by region and country. Women's share approaches parity with that of men (i.e., is in the range of 45-55%) primarily in Western Europe and Other Developed Countries, Eastern Europe and Latin America. The share appears to be influenced by economic structure: If agriculture is the primary means of livelihood, women's share of non-agricultural employment is small. Where non-agricultural wage work plays a greater role in the economy, women's share is higher.

Work in industry and services usually puts some money directly into the hands of women, unlike employ-

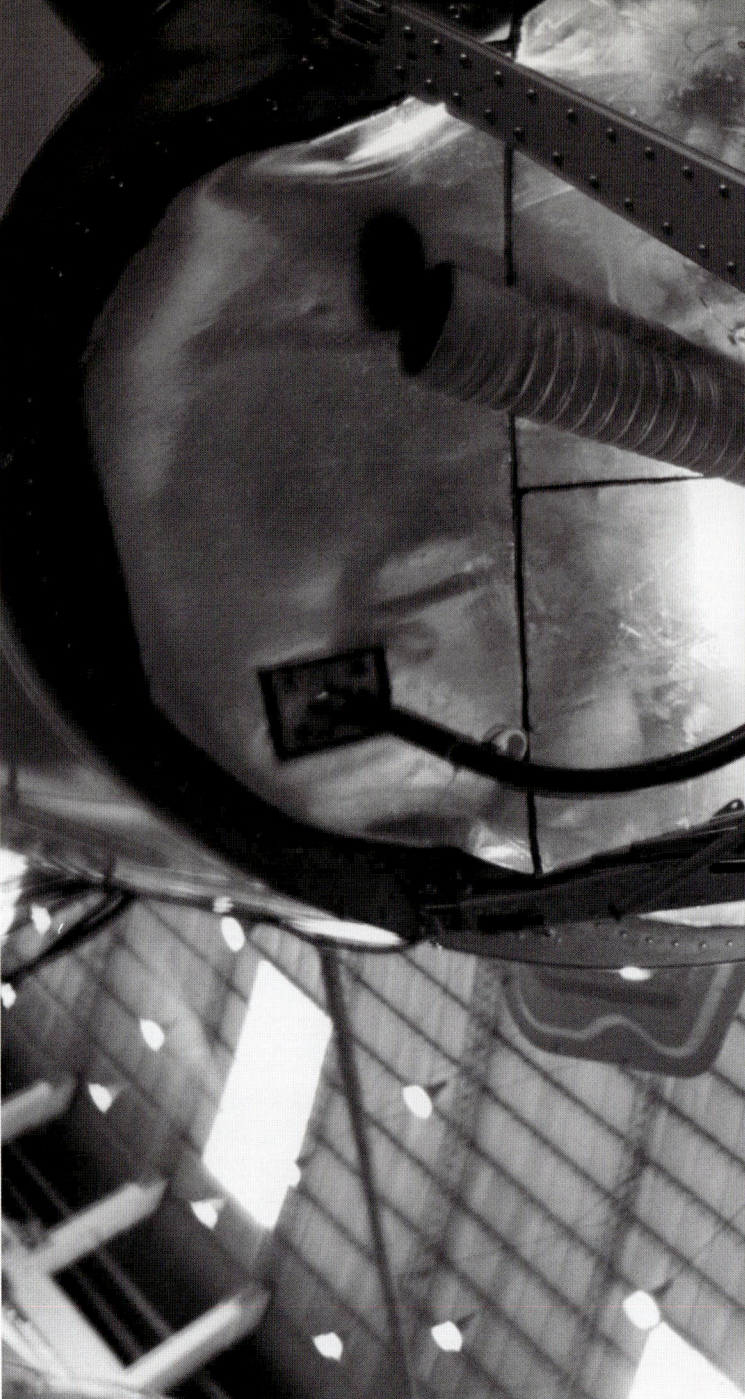

ment on a family farm or unpaid work in a family business. Moreover, the pay is likely to be higher than the average pay for self-employment. Still, waged work is often neither secure nor well paid for the majority of people around the world. Economists generally make a distinction between 'formal' wage work which is often reasonably well paid, secure and performed in safe and healthy conditions versus 'informal' wage work, which is likely to be unregulated, poorly paid, lacking job security, dangerous — and frequently performed by women.

Because of the unregulated nature of informal wage work it is not fully covered in government surveys, so that we have only a partial picture of women's wage employment.

In general, there is far less data available for the MDG female employment indicator than for education and literacy, and that data is not up to date for a large number of countries, especially in sub-

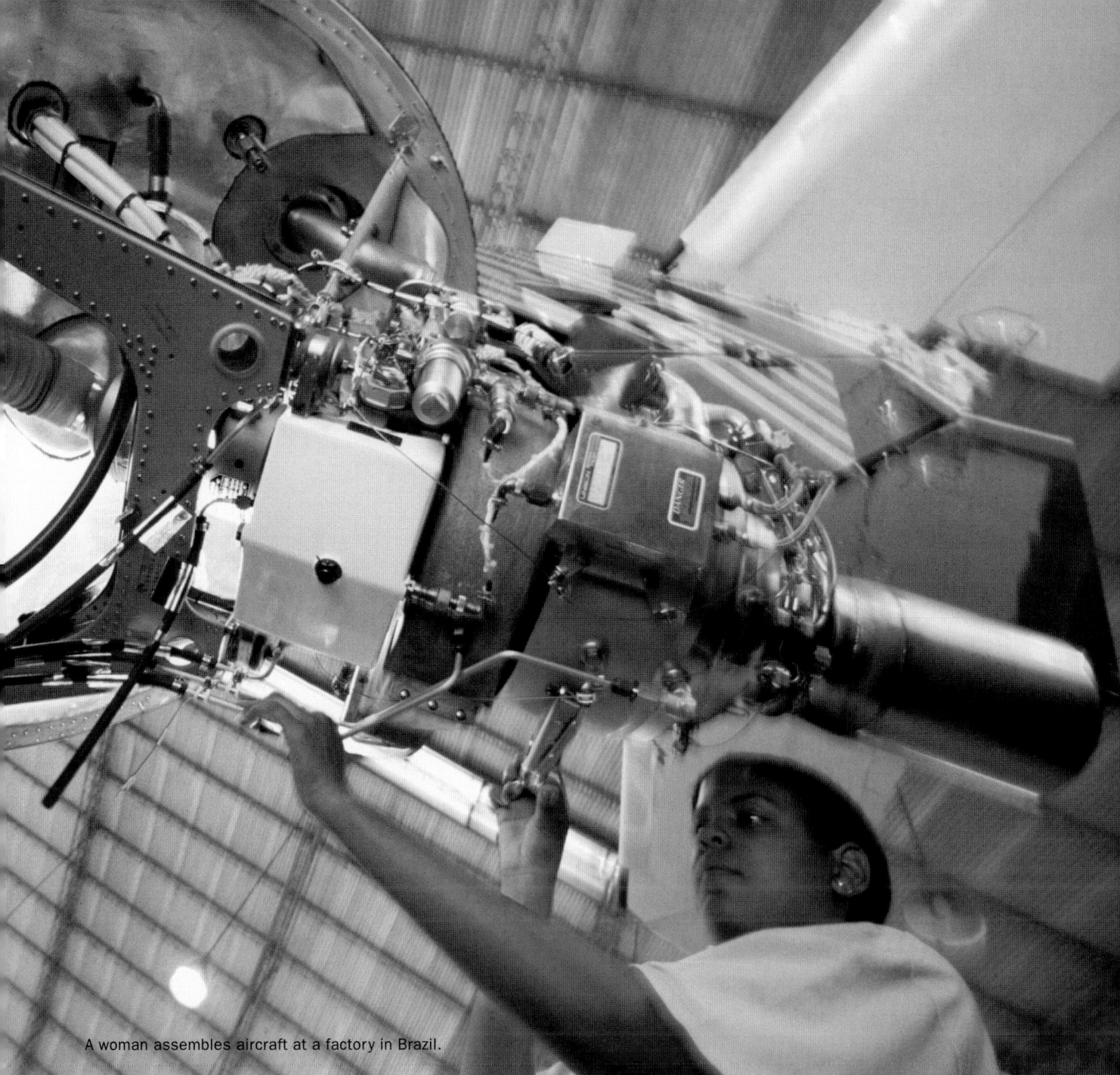

A woman assembles aircraft at a factory in Brazil.

Saharan and Northern Africa.

The ILO has data for only 13 out of 53 countries in Africa, and out of these there is recent data for only four. That data shows a wide range, from Botswana where women have 47 per cent of the non-agricultural paid employment, to Chad where they have only 6 per cent. The number is low in Chad partly because so many women are in agricultural employment, but also because 95 per cent of women's non-agricultural employment is informal (compared with 60 per cent for men), and 99 per cent of this informal employment is self-employment (the figure for men is 86%). Neither of these types of employment are reflected in the data (see Tables 5 and 6, pp. 38-39).

In Central and Western Asia there is data for only seven out of 22 countries. The range is also wide, from Kazakhstan with equal shares of men and women in non-agricultural paid employment, to Turkey where women's share is only 10 per cent. But this figure underestimates women's share because it is based on social insurance records and many women workers in Turkey are not eligible for this insurance for a variety of reasons.

In Asia and the Pacific, data is available for 12 out of 27 countries. Women's share ranges from 47 per cent to 30 per cent, except in South Asia. There, the low figures (everywhere but Sri Lanka) reflect a situation similar to Chad: In India, for example, a high proportion of women's employment is in agriculture. And for those women in non-agricultural employment, a higher proportion of them than of men are in the informal sector, primarily as self-employed workers (see Tables 5 and 6).

In all the other regions of the world, more data is

available and it is more up to date. In these regions there is no country (of those for which data is available) in which women have less than a 30 per cent share. In Latin America and the Caribbean, the shares range from Jamaica where women have parity with men, to El Salvador where women's share is 32 per cent. In Eastern Europe, there is a small 'reverse' gender gap in six countries, with women's share at slightly more than half. In Western Europe and Other Developed Countries, two countries have a reverse gender gap.

Changes in Women's Share

Chart 4 (pp. 34-36) shows changes in the female share, comparing the early 1980s, mid-1990s and the latest available data, although there is not much data on recent changes, except for Eastern Europe and Western Europe and Other Developed Countries. In 54 countries, women's share is increasing; in six it is going down.

In sub-Saharan and Northern Africa, there is an upward trend in the six countries for which data is available, except for Malawi, which has leveled off. There is a similar upward trend in all areas of Central and Western Asia, except for Turkey, and in Asia and the Pacific, except for the Philippines and the Republic of Korea. In the Philippines, women's share fell from 48 per cent in the early 1980s to 40 per cent in the mid-1990s and only slightly recovered to 41 per cent by 2000. In the Republic of Korea, women's share rose from 36 per cent to 39 per cent by the mid-1990s, and then fell one percentage point in 2000. The drops in women's share in both countries was probably due to financial crises, which led to the growth of informal employment for women.

In Latin America and the Caribbean as well as in Eastern Europe, trends have been mixed. There is an upward trend in Brazil, Costa Rica and Trinidad and Tobago. In Panama, the share rose and then fell below the previous level, while in Venezuela it rose and then stayed constant. Meanwhile, in Eastern Europe, there is an upward trend in the Czech Republic, the Former Yugoslav Republic of Macedonia, Slovakia and Slovenia, but in Estonia and Lithuania women's share fell in the mid-1990s and has not recovered. In Western Europe and Other Developed countries, there has been an upward trend in ten countries and a leveling off in seven, three of which had already reached parity. As countries approach parity they naturally tend to level off in this way.

Analysing Informal, Insecure Employment

Because the indicator for women's share of non-agricultural employment provides only limited information on women's paid work, various agencies and NGOs have proposed additional indicators that may help to provide a more complete picture. For a start, informal work must be more closely charted. The ILO has proposed a set of definitions for informal workers that include:

- workers who have no contract of [CONTINUED ON PAGE 37]

Table 4: Female Share of Wage

SUB-SAHARAN AFRICA

Country	Year	Female Share (%)
Botswana	1998	47
Mauritius	2000	38
Swaziland	1996	33
Kenya	1997	32
Eritrea	1996	31
Ethiopia	1993	28
Côte d'Ivoire	1990	23
Sudan	1991	20
Zimbabwe	1999	19
Burkina Faso	1992	12
Malawi	1995	11
Niger	1991	9
Chad	1991	6

NORTHERN AFRICA

Country	Year	Female Share (%)
Egypt	1999	21

CENTRAL AND WESTERN ASIA

Country	Year	Female Share (%)
Kazakhstan	1998	50
Israel	2000	48
Cyprus	2000	44
Jordan	1993	23
Bahrain	2000	12
Syria	1991	11
Turkey	1998	10

ASIA AND THE PACIFIC

Country	Year	Female Share (%)
Thailand	2000	47
Sri Lanka	2000	46
Hong Kong, China	2001	45
Singapore	1999	45
Philippines	2000	41
China	1999	40
Korea, Rep.	2000	38
Indonesia	1990	38
Malaysia	1993	36
Fiji	1996	32
India	1998	16
Pakistan	1994	8

Employment in Non-Agricultural Sector, Latest Available Data

LATIN AMERICA AND THE CARIBBEAN

Country	Year	Female Share (%)
Jamaica	1992	50
Colombia	2000	49
Bahamas	1994	49
Barbados	1994	47
Honduras	1992	47
Brazil	1999	45
Argentina	2000	43
Panama	1999	42
Trinidad & Tobago	1999	40
Costa Rica	2000	39
Mexico	2000	37
Bolivia	1996	37
Chile	1999	36
Venezuela	1993	35
Peru	2000	33
El Salvador	1996	32

EASTERN EUROPE

Country	Year	Female Share (%)
Ukraine	2000	53
Lithuania	2000	53
Bulgaria	1999	52
Latvia	2000	51
Estonia	2000	51
Slovakia	1999	51
Slovenia	1999	48
Poland	2000	47
Czech Rep	2000	47
Croatia	2000	47
Hungary	2001	46
Romania	2000	45
Macedonia FYR	1999	41
Albania	1991	41

WESTERN EUROPE AND OTHER DEVELOPED COUNTRIES

Country	Year	Female Share (%)
Iceland	2000	52
Sweden	2000	51
United Kingdom	2000	50
New Zealand	2000	50
Finland	2000	50
Denmark	2000	49
USA	2000	48
Norway	2000	48
Canada	2000	48
Portugal	2000	46
France	2000	46
Ireland	1999	46
Germany	2000	45
Australia	1996	45
Netherlands	2000	44
Belgium	1999	44
Switzerland	2000	42
Austria	1993	41
Spain	2000	40
Japan	2000	40
Italy	2000	40
Greece	2000	40
Luxembourg	1998	36
Malta	1999	31

Source: ILO website; http://laborsta.ilo.org

CHART 4: Changes in Female Share of Wage Employment in Non-Agricultural Sector, Early 1980s, Mid-1990s, Latest Available Data

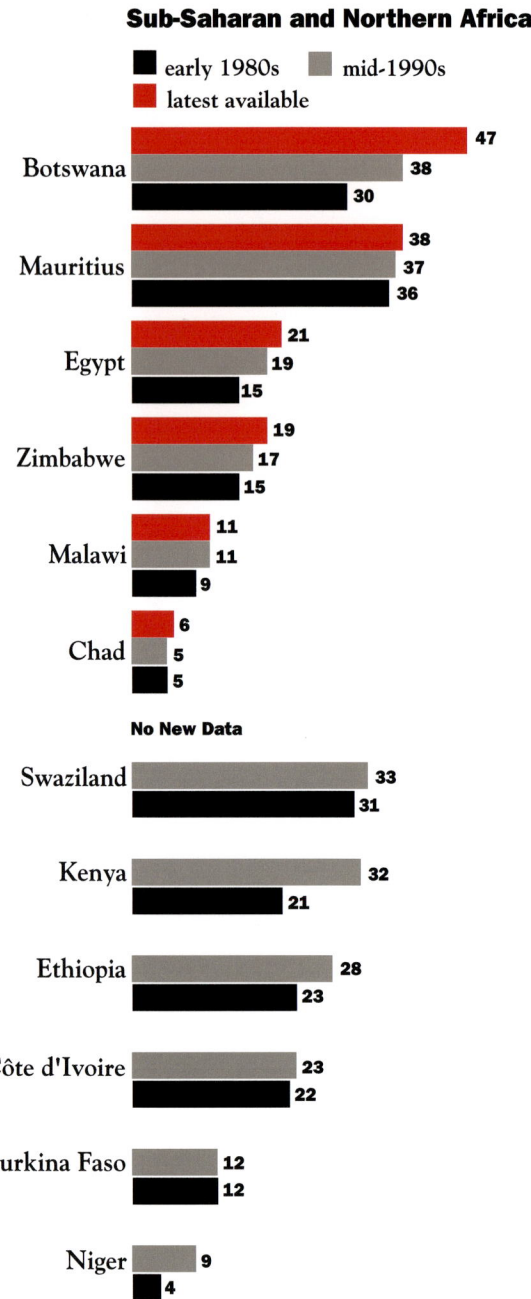

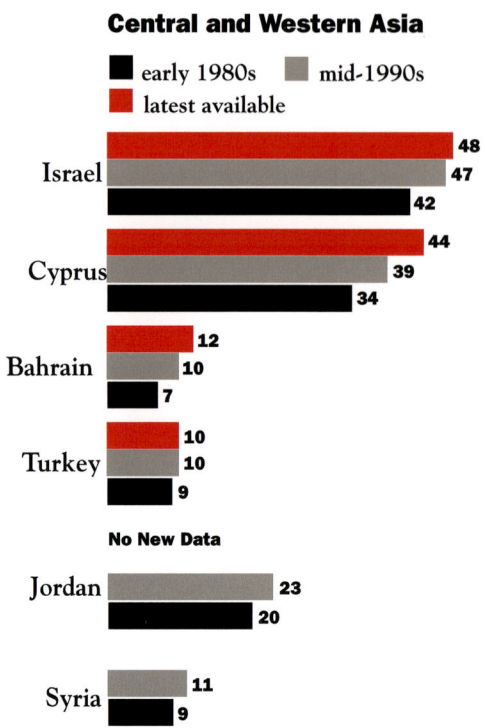

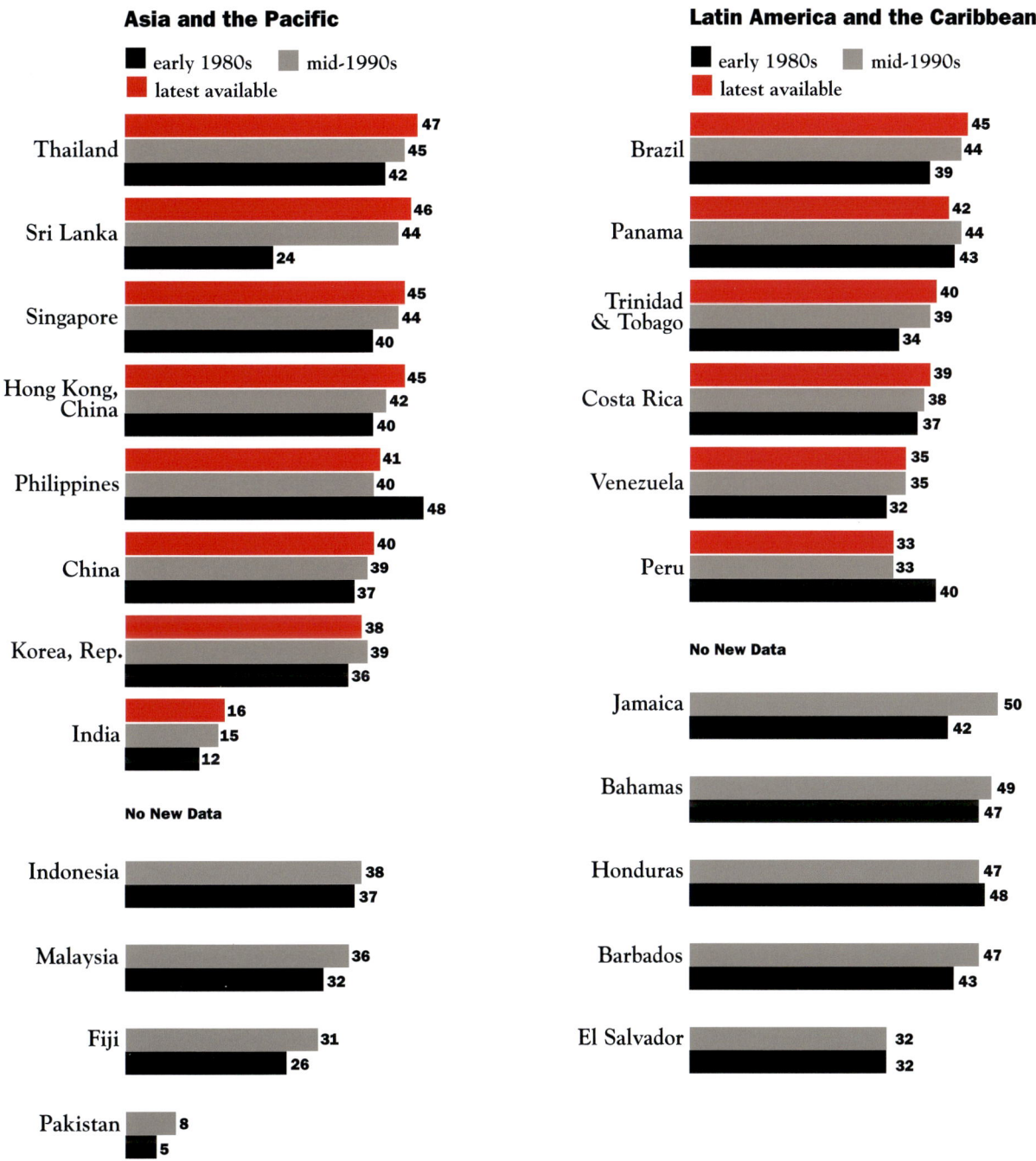

[CHART CONTINUED ON PAGE 36]

CHART 4: Changes in Female Share of Wage Employment in Non-Agricultural Sector, Early 1980s, Mid-1990s, Latest Available Data (cont'd.)

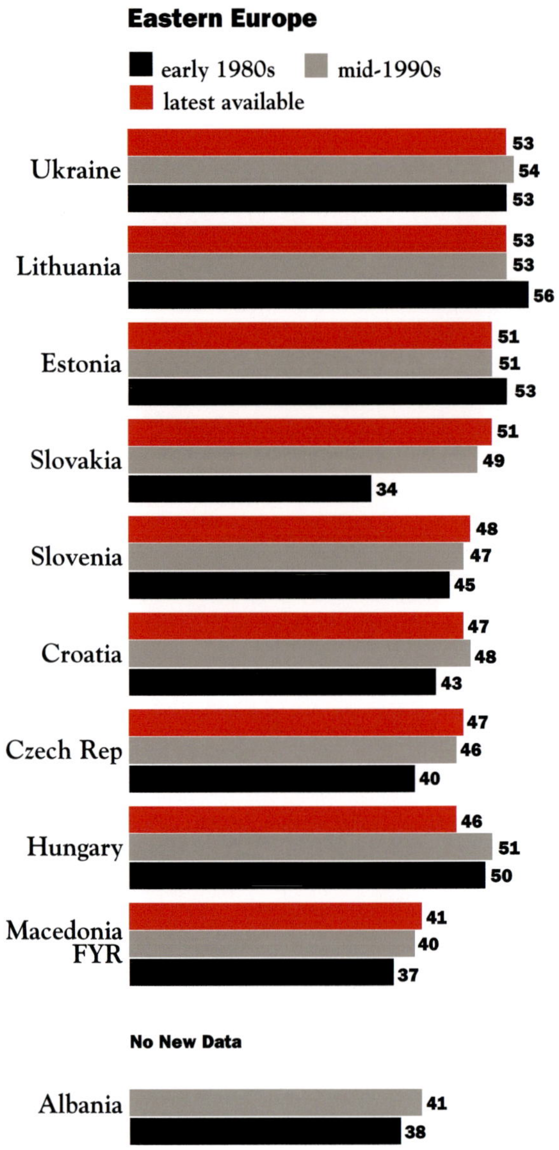

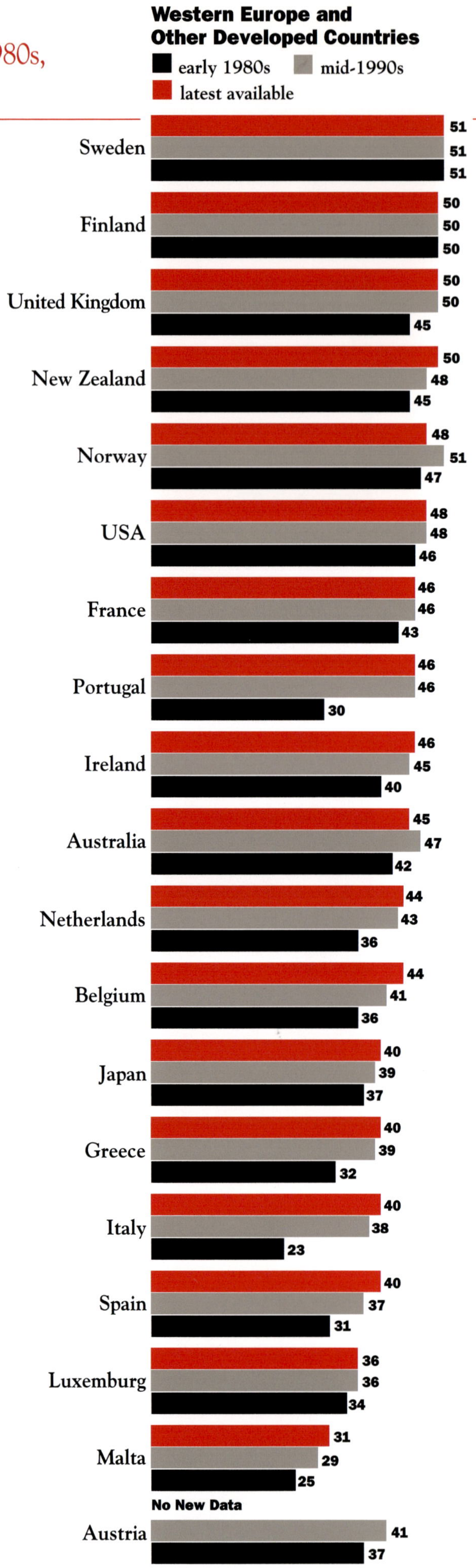

Eastern Europe

■ early 1980s   ■ mid-1990s   ■ latest available

Country	early 1980s	mid-1990s	latest available
Ukraine	53	54	53
Lithuania	56	53	53
Estonia	53	51	51
Slovakia	34	49	51
Slovenia	45	47	48
Croatia	43	48	47
Czech Rep	40	46	47
Hungary	50	51	46
Macedonia FYR	37	40	41

No New Data

Country	early 1980s	mid-1990s
Albania	38	41

Western Europe and Other Developed Countries

■ early 1980s   ■ mid-1990s   ■ latest available

Country	early 1980s	mid-1990s	latest available
Sweden	51	51	51
Finland	50	50	50
United Kingdom	45	50	50
New Zealand	45	48	50
Norway	47	51	48
USA	46	48	48
France	43	46	46
Portugal	30	46	46
Ireland	40	45	46
Australia	42	47	45
Netherlands	36	43	44
Belgium	36	41	44
Japan	37	39	40
Greece	32	39	40
Italy	23	38	40
Spain	31	37	40
Luxemburg	34	36	36
Malta	25	29	31

No New Data

Country	early 1980s	mid-1990s
Austria	37	41

Source: ILO website; http://laborsta.ilo.org

36 • ASSESSING PROGRESS

[CONTINUED FROM PAGE 32] employment and no legal or social protection arising from the job, whether they work in the formal sector of the economy (factories that offer daily work, for example, as well as contract work) or the informal sector
- self-employed or 'own-account' workers and employers who have their own informal enterprises
- members of informal producers' cooperatives
- producers of goods for final use by their households (e.g., subsistence farming)
- paid domestic workers employed by households in informal jobs

Table 5 (p. 38) shows estimates of the share of informal employment (both waged and self-employed) in non-agricultural employment in the 1990s for a group of developing countries. It is clear that in many countries informal employment is a high proportion of non-agricultural employment. In sub-Saharan Africa and Latin America, women's informal employment as a percentage of their non-agricultural employment is higher than the corresponding figure for men.

Table 6 (p. 39) shows that much of women's informal employment is self-employment rather than wage work. In fact, in developing countries in all regions, self-employment is the largest share of informal employment for both women and men and appears to be on the increase. According to the ILO,

> Between 1980 and 2000 self-employment increased from about one-quarter to about one-third of non-agricultural employment worldwide. Self-employment in non-agricultural activities increased in almost all developing regions. However, declines occurred in Eastern Europe where it dropped sharply, from 18 to 9 per cent of non-agricultural employment; and in Eastern Asia, where it dropped from 23 to 18 per cent (ILO 2002a:22).

Although the percentage of self-employment is increasing among both women and men, the proportion of women in non-agricultural work who are self-employed is increasing faster than the proportion for men. Worldwide, women's share increased from 28 per cent to 34 per cent between 1980 and 2000 while that for men increased from 25 per cent to only 27 per cent. There are many questions about the increase in informal and self-employed wage work for women: Is this increase beneficial? Are the benefits shared equally by women and men? Why is women's share of self-employment growing faster than men's? The answers will require more sophisticated statistics-gathering, models for which are being developed with support from UN agencies such as the ILO, UNDP, and UNIFEM.

As part of the effort to better understand the entire range of waged employment, the ILO is constructing a set of 'Decent Work' indicators (see Box 6, p. 38).

Should There Be a New Target?

Currently, there is no MDG target for gender equality in the labour market. Various individuals and groups have argued that an additional target is necessary since school enrolment alone does not address women's equality and empowerment. They have proposed that this additional target look at wage disparity. The Economic Commission for Latin America and the Caribbean (ECLAC) has proposed such a target that would seek to:

> "Significantly reduce wage differences between women and men with the same level of skills."
> To be measured by the ratio of women's to men's average wages by years of schooling.
> (ECLAC 2002:7)

While we believe this is a good step forward, the indicator (the ratio of women's to men's average wages by years of schooling) is hampered by the same problem as the gender disparity indicators for education and literacy: It is possible to reduce the gender wage gap by pushing men's wages down instead of increasing women's, as has occurred in the United States in recent years. To track whether the wage gap is reduced through equality in prosperity, it would help to include an indicator suggested by a recent ILO paper (Anker et al. 2002): the percentage of workers with gross hourly earnings that are less than half the median value of hourly earnings in the country concerned. The median value divides the distribution of earnings in two, so that 50 per cent of earners receive below the median pay and 50 per cent receive above it. A person who gets less than half the median can reasonably be considered a person with low pay. By measuring what percentage of women workers earn less than half the median compared to the percentage of men, it would be possible to identify and analyse gender disparities in the labour market.

Another, simpler, indicator might be the percentage of women and men with hourly earnings below what is considered a 'living wage,' although defining 'living wage' has not been easy. One possibility discussed by Anker et al. would be to take the World Bank poverty rate of $2 a day as a starting point, and then to assume that a living wage should allow a worker to earn more than $2 a day and support at least one other person besides themselves, working eight hours a day, six days a week, 50 weeks a year. This is a very minimum level of living since "this ...assumes long hours, a small dependency ratio and a poverty level income requirement" (Anker et al. 2002:29).

Reducing gender disparity in the economy is such an important issue that UN agencies should work together to set targets and improve indicators at regional and national levels, taking into account the differences in economic structures in different parts of the world.

BOX 6: ILO DECENT WORK INDICATORS

These indicators will be created through the use of a People's Security Survey conducted with 2,000-3,000 households in a variety of countries. The survey asks household members a broad range of questions about wage work, from salary to working conditions to job security to hours of work. In November 2001, a prototype index was presented, which drew on the Indonesian People's Security Survey. The Indonesian survey showed that while both men and women have a low average score for secure, decent work, women's score is lower. The gender gap increases as household income rises: Men's work is generally more secure than women's. In poorer, more vulnerable households, both men and women are equally at the mercy of the vagaries of the job market, with little protection from layoffs or reduced wages and few if any benefits.

Results for Argentina, Bangladesh, Brazil, Chile, China, Ethiopia, Ghana, India, Indonesia, Hungary, Pakistan, Russia, South Africa, Tanzania and Ukraine will be available through a series of ILO publications.

Sources: www.ilo.org
ILO 2002b

Table 5: Informal Employment in Non-Agricultural Employment, by Sex, 1994-2000

Region/Country	Informal Employment as % of Non-Agricultural Employment	Women's Informal Employment as % of Non-Agricultural Employment	Men's Informal Employment as % of Non-Agricultural Employment
North Africa	**48**	**43**	**49**
Algeria	43	41	43
Morocco	45	47	44
Tunisia	50	39	53
Egypt	55	46	57
Sub-Saharan Africa	**72**	**84**	**63**
Benin	93	97	87
Chad	74	95	60
Guinea	72	87	66
Kenya	72	83	59
South Africa	51	58	44
Latin America	**51**	**58**	**48**
Bolivia	63	74	55
Brazil	60	67	55
Chile	36	44	31
Colombia	38	44	34
Costa Rica	44	48	42
El Salvador	57	69	46
Guatemala	56	69	47
Honduras	58	65	74
Mexico	55	55	54
Dominican Republic	72	84	63
Venezuela	47	47	47
Asia	**65**	**65**	**65**
India	83	86	83
Indonesia	78	77	78
Philippines	72	73	71
Thailand	51	54	49
Syria	42	35	43

Source: ILO, Women and Men in the Informal Economy: A Statistical Picture, Geneva 2002a

Table 6: Wage and Self-Employment in Non-Agricultural Informal Employment, by Sex 1994-2000

Region/Country	Self-Employment as % of Non-Agricultural Informal Employment			Wage Employment as % of Non-Agricultural Informal Employment		
	Total	Women	Men	Total	Women	Men
North Africa	**62**	**72**	**60**	**38**	**28**	**40**
Algeria	67	81	64	33	19	36
Morocco	81	89	78	19	11	22
Tunisia	52	51	52	48	49	48
Egypt	50	67	47	50	33	53
Sub-Saharan Africa	**70**	**71**	**70**	**30**	**29**	**30**
Benin	95	98	91	5	2	9
Chad	93	99	86	7	1	14
Guinea	95	98	94	5	2	6
Kenya	42	33	56	58	67	44
South Africa	25	27	23	75	73	77
Latin America	**60**	**58**	**61**	**40**	**42**	**39**
Bolivia	81	91	71	19	9	29
Brazil	41	32	50	59	68	50
Chile	52	39	64	48	61	36
Colombia	38	36	40	62	64	60
Costa Rica	55	49	59	45	54	41
El Salvador	65	71	57	35	29	43
Guatemala	60	65	55	40	35	45
Honduras	72	77	65	28	23	35
Mexico	54	53	54	46	47	46
Dominican Republic	74	63	80	26	37	20
Venezuela	69	66	70	31	34	30
Asia	**59**	**63**	**55**	**41**	**37**	**45**
India	52	57	51	48	43	49
Indonesia	63	70	59	37	30	41
Philippines	48	63	36	52	37	64
Thailand	66	68	64	34	32	36
Syria	65	57	67	35	43	33

Source: ILO, *Women and Men in the Informal Economy: A Statistical Picture*, Geneva 2002a

SEATS IN PARLIAMENT

Key Findings

- Around the world women are largely absent from parliaments, on average accounting for only about 14 per cent of members in 2002. There are no systematic differences between rich and poor countries, and considerable variations within each region.
- In 2002, only 11 countries had achieved the benchmark set in the Beijing Platform for Action of 30 per cent representation by women in parliament: Sweden, Denmark, Germany, Finland, Norway, Iceland, the Netherlands, South Africa, Costa Rica, Argentina and Mozambique. In all of these countries quotas were legislated or adopted on a voluntary basis.
- New Zealand just missed the target with women's representation in parliament at 29.2 per cent after its most recent election.
- Nevertheless, there was continued progress in all regions between 2000 and 2002 towards the benchmark.
- Women's share of seats in parliament fell in 22 countries. Particularly disappointing were two cases in which a return to democracy was accompanied by a reduction in women's representation. In Nigeria women's share of seats fell to a very disappointing 3.2 per cent. In Indonesia women's share fell from 11.4 per cent to only 8 per cent.
- The large fall in women's share of seats which followed the transition to market economies in Eastern Europe has been reversed in three countries: Bulgaria, the Former Yugoslav Republic of Macedonia and Poland.
- In some rich countries, women's representation in the legislature remains well below that achieved in many poor countries. Women's share of seats in the United States is 12 per cent but 38 developing countries have a higher share.

The Gender Gap in Representation in Parliament

The empowerment of women requires that women have more say in all the decisions that affect their lives, including in the household, the community, the market place, the workplace, and in all levels of public assemblies and offices, from the local to the national to the international. It is difficult to produce global estimates of the degree to which women have enhanced their position in all these arenas. The only indicator that can currently be tabulated for the world as a whole is women's share of seats in national parliaments. Although it does not truly cover the breadth of women's involvement in decision-making, it is nevertheless useful.

The goal of increasing women's representation in parliaments is a long-standing one, and was agreed upon at numerous international conferences prior to the Millennium Summit. The target of 30 per cent representation in key decision-making positions was endorsed by the UN Economic and Social Council and was reiterated in the 1995 Beijing Platform for Action (para. 182). Women in many parts of the world have been campaigning to meet this target, and to go beyond it to achieve true parity (see Box 7, p. 42).

But increasing women's share of seats in parliament is not a panacea. It can only level the playing field on which women battle for equality. While women the world over campaign for equal representation, most recognize that this is not, and never can be, a guarantee that women in power will make decisions that benefit the majority of women. And beyond the personal perspectives of individual candidates, many other factors prevent them from promoting laws and programmes that aid women: The power of parliamentarians may be limited by the decisions of international investors; by the rules of international bodies such as the World Trade Organization (WTO); by the loan conditions of international financial institutions such as the World Bank and the International Monetary Fund (IMF); by national constitutions that hamper parliamentary power in relation to the executive powers of government; and by political parties that exert strong discipline over their members. Despite all this, women's presence is essential: Their absence from national legislatures signals that women are not accepted as equal partners in political decision-making for the nation.

Women's presence is especially important in post-conflict situations, when new constitutions and new parliaments are often being created. Until recently women were almost completely excluded from peace-building and post-war decision-making. Now, with the support of UNIFEM and many other organizations, the issue of women's participation is receiving more attention. The UN Security Council adopted Resolution 1325 in October 2000 urging Member States to increase women's representation at all levels of decision-making institutions for preventing, managing and resolving conflict. It calls on all actors negotiating and implementing peace agreements to adopt a gender perspective and to include women in implementing mechanisms of the peace agreement. Since then, women have been included in the decision-making mechanisms setting up the new Democratic Republic of East Timor. In August 2001 elections were held to set up a Constituent Assembly, with women gaining 26.1 per cent of the votes. This body became the national parliament on 20 May 2002, when East Timor officially became independent.

Table 7 (pp. 42-43) gives a regional and country breakdown of women's share of seats in national parliaments in November 2002, based on the data compiled by the Inter-Parliamentary Union (IPU).

Changes in Women's Share

There has been continued progress towards the 30 per cent benchmark in recent elections in a significant

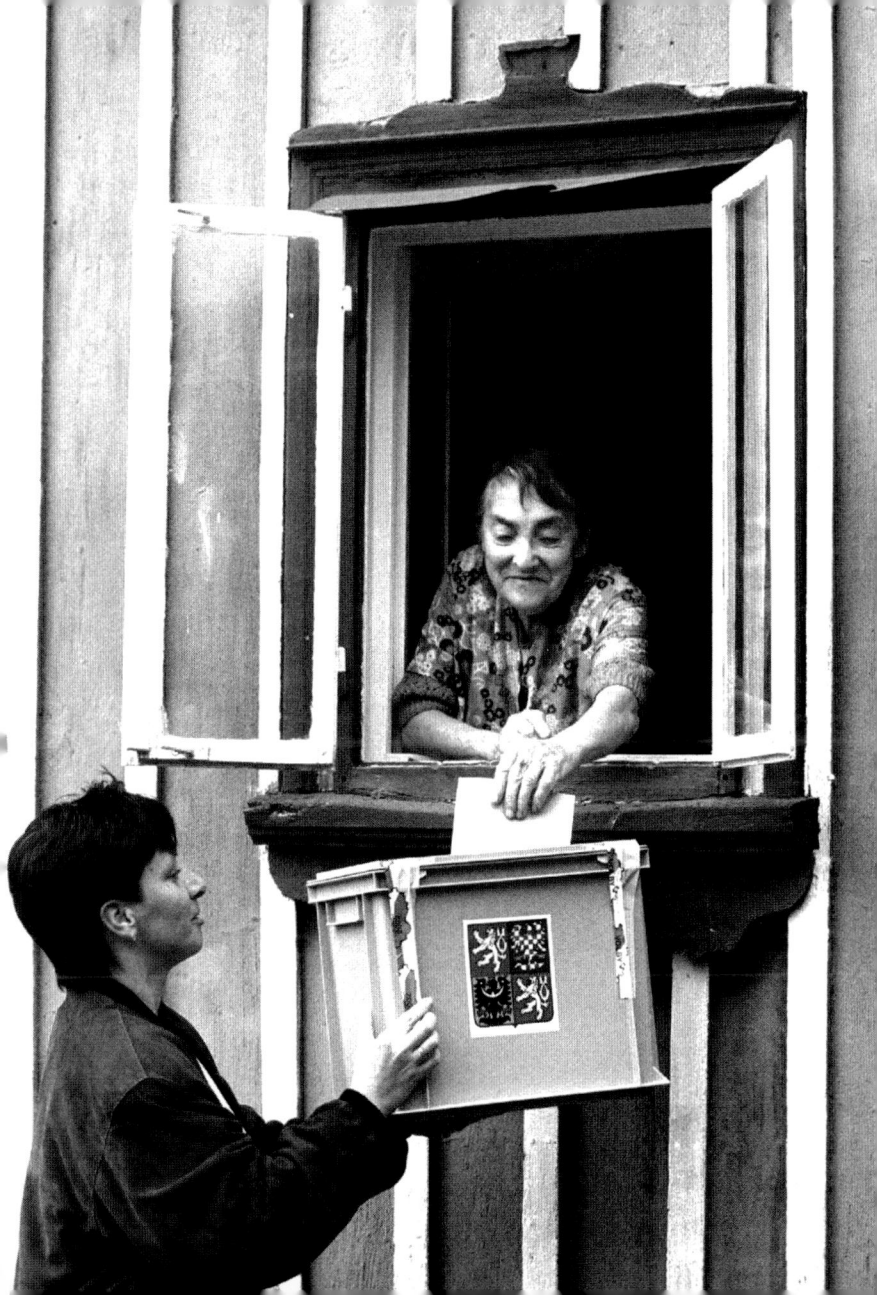

Table 7: Women's Share of Seats in National Parliament, November

SUB-SAHARAN AFRICA	(%)
South Africa	30.0
Mozambique	30.0
Rwanda	25.7
Uganda	24.7
Seychelles	23.5
Tanzania, UR	22.3
Namibia	20.0
Burundi	19.5
Senegal	19.2
Botswana	17.0
Angola	15.5
Eritrea	14.7
Mali	12.2
Congo	12.0
Zambia	12.0
Cape Verde	11.1
Liberia	11.1
Gabon	10.9
Lesotho	10.7
Zimbabwe	10.0
Burkina Faso	9.9
Sudan	9.7
Malawi	9.3
Ghana	9.0
Cameroon	8.9
Guinea	8.8
Côte d'Ivoire	8.5
Madagascar	8.0
Guinea-Bissau	7.8
Ethiopia	7.8
Central African Rep.	7.3
Swaziland	6.3
Benin	6.0
Mauritius	5.7
Gambia	5.7
Cameroon	5.6
Eq. Guinea	5.0
Togo	4.9
Kenya	3.6
Nigeria	3.2
Mauritania	1.8
Niger	1.2
Djibouti	0.0

NORTHERN AFRICA	(%)
Tunisia	11.5
Algeria	4.0
Egypt	2.4
Morocco	0.5

CENTRAL AND WESTERN ASIA	(%)
Turkmenistan	26.0
Israel	14.2
Tajikistan	12.0
Kazakhstan	11.2
Cyprus	10.7
Azerbaijan	10.5
Syria	10.4
Iraq	7.6
Uzbekistan	7.2
Georgia	7.2
Kyrgyzstan	6.6
Turkey	4.2
Jordan	3.3
Armenia	3.1
Lebanon	2.3
Yemen	0.7

ASIA AND THE PACIFIC	(%)
Viet Nam	27.3
East Timor, DR	26.1
Lao PDR	22.9
China	21.8
Korea, DPR	20.1
Philippines	17.0
Malaysia	14.5
Singapore	11.0
Mongolia	10.5
Thailand	9.6
Cambodia	9.3
Bhutan	9.3
India	8.9
Indonesia	8.0
Maldives	6.0
Samoa (Western)	6.1
Nepal	5.9
Korea, Rep.	5.9
Fiji	5.7
Sri Lanka	4.4
Iran, Islamic Rep.	4.1
Bangladesh	2.0
Vanuatu	1.9

2002

LATIN AMERICA AND THE CARIBBEAN

	(%)
Costa Rica	31.6
Argentina	31.3
Cuba	27.6
Nicaragua	20.7
Barbados	20.4
Guyana	20.0
Suriname	17.6
Peru	17.5
Trinidad & Tobago	16.7
Mexico	16.0
Jamaica	16.0
Dominican Rep.	15.4
Ecuador	14.6
Belize	13.5
Uruguay	12.0
Colombia	11.0
Bolivia	10.2
Chile	10.0
Panama	9.9
Venezuela	9.7
El Salvador	9.5
Haiti	9.0
Guatemala	8.8
Paraguay	8.0
Brazil	6.7
Honduras	5.5

EASTERN EUROPE

	(%)
Bulgaria	26.2
Poland	21.0
Belarus	18.3
Latvia	18.0
Estonia	17.8
Macedonia, FYR	17.5
Croatia	16.0
Czech Rep.	15.6
Slovakia	14.0
Moldova, Rep.	12.9
Slovenia	12.2
Lithuania	10.6
Romania	9.2
Hungary	9.1
Russian Fed.	6.4
Bosnia-Herzegovina	6.4
Yugoslavia	6.2
Albania	5.7
Ukraine	5.1*

WESTERN EUROPE AND OTHER DEVELOPED COUNTRIES

	(%)
Sweden	42.7
Denmark	38.0
Finland	36.5
Norway	36.4
Iceland	34.9
Netherlands	31.5
Germany	31.0
New Zealand	30.8
Australia	27.0
Spain	26.6
Austria	25.1
Belgium	24.8
Canada	24.0
Switzerland	22.0
Portugal	19.1
United Kingdom	17.0
Luxembourg	16.7
Ireland	14.6
United States	12.0
France	11.8
Japan	10.0
Malta	9.2
Italy	9.1
Greece	8.7

Sources: Inter-Parliamentary Union
website: http://www.ipu.org
*www.uatoday.net

CHART 5: Changes in Women's Share of Seats in

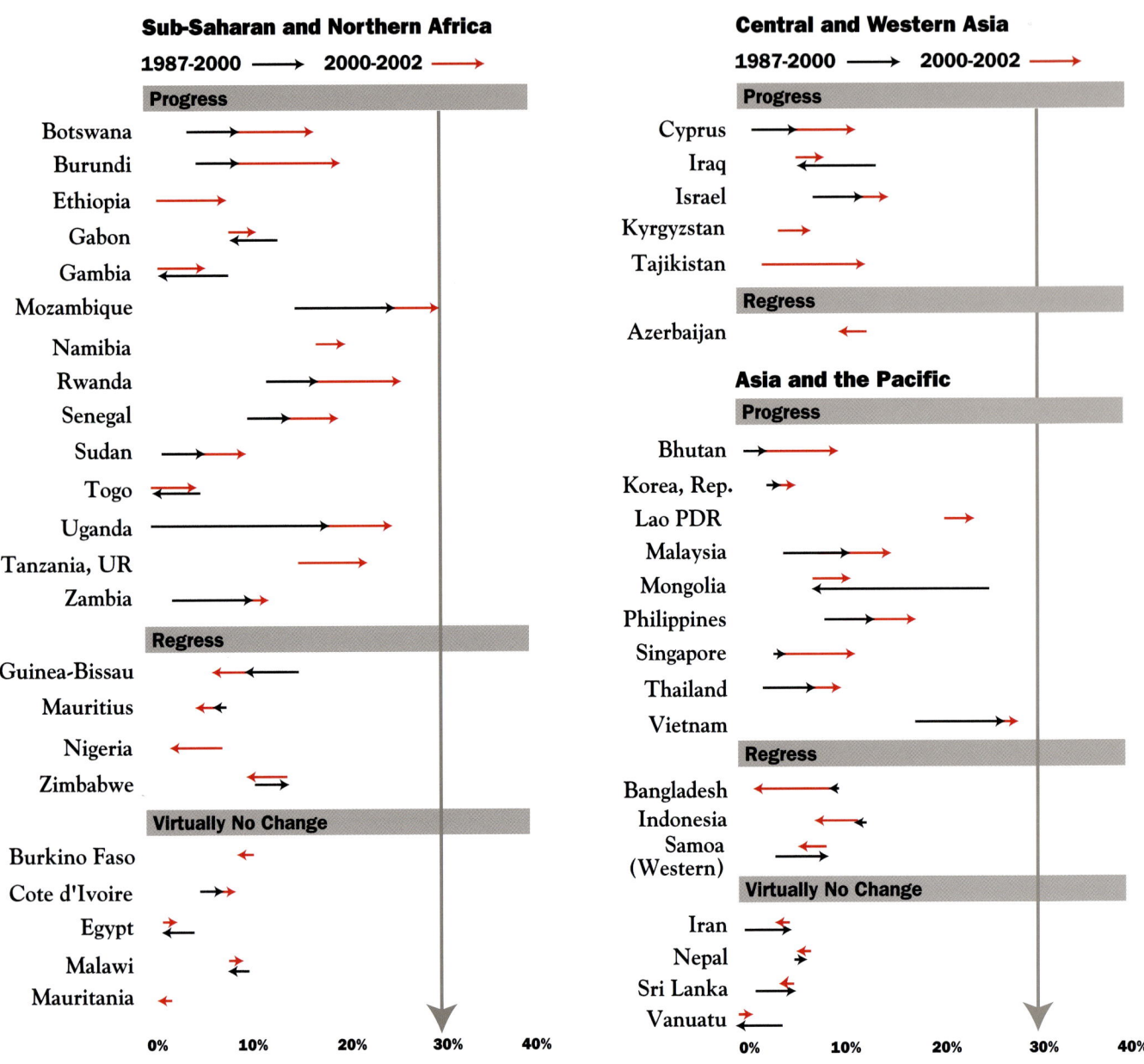

National Parliament, 1987-2000-2002

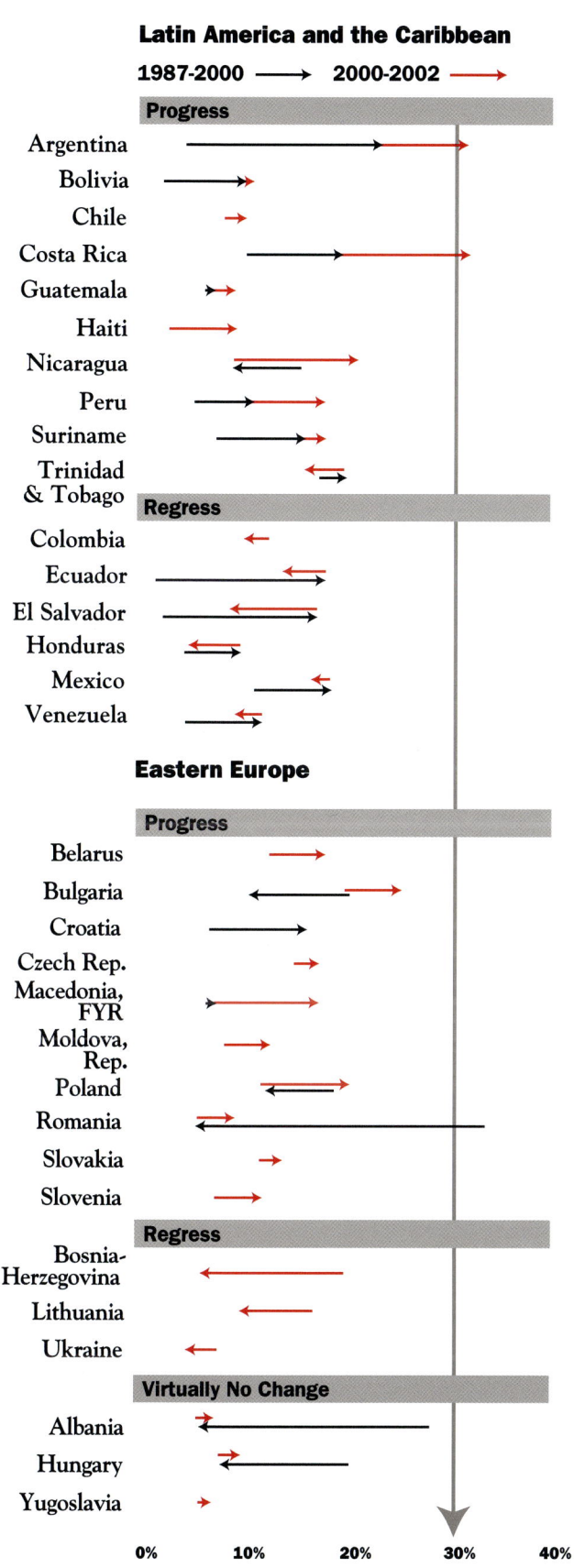

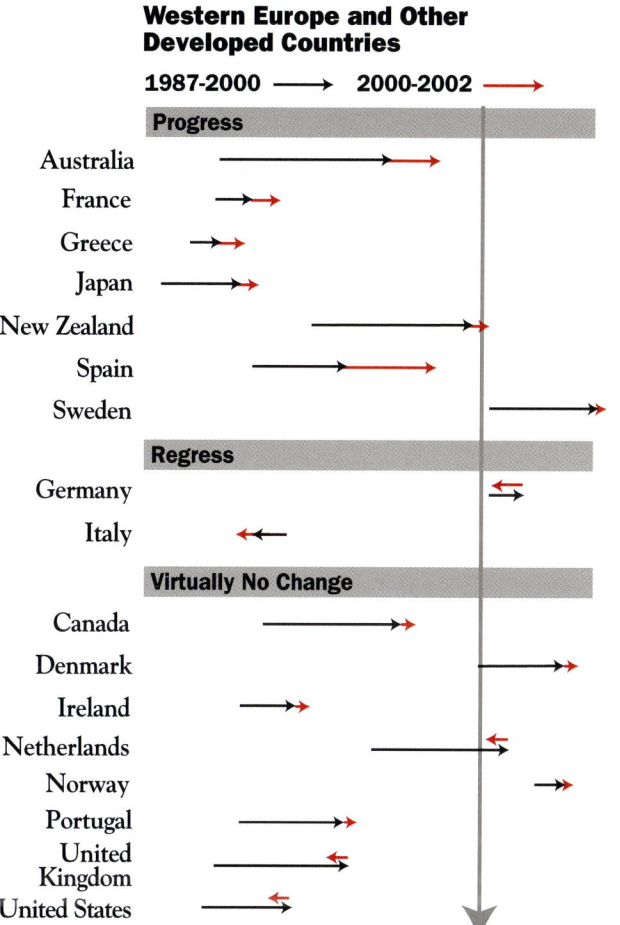

Progress: Increase of more than 1 percentage point
Regress: Decrease of more than -1 percentage point
Virtually No Change: Change in range +1 to -1 percentage points

Sources: Inter-Parliamentary Union Website: http://www.ipu.org;
The World's Women 1995: Trends and Statistics. 2nd ed.
New York: UN Statistical Division.

> **BOX 7: THE 50/50 CAMPAIGN: GET THE BALANCE RIGHT!**
>
> *Worldwide, women make up more than half the population, but they hold only 12.7 percent of all parliamentary seats. What's wrong with these numbers?*
>
> *No government can claim to be democratic until women are guaranteed the right to equal representation. At the 1995 Beijing Fourth World Conference on Women, 189 governments agreed to this principle in the Beijing Platform, and committed themselves to take steps to achieve it.*
>
> *But the percentage of women legislators has only increased .5 percent a year since then. At that rate, it would take 75 years to reach an equal gender balance!*
>
> WEDO 50/50 Campaign www.wedo.org
>
> The Women's Environment and Development Organization (WEDO) launched its 50/50 campaign in 2000, during the five-year review of the Beijing Platform for Action (PFA). The campaign's goals are to take the target of 30 per cent in the PFA and push it to true gender equality: 50/50 representation between women and men. The campaign is working to increase the percentage of women in local and national legislatures worldwide through education, training potential candidates and meetings with political leaders. It has been adopted by 154 organizations in 45 countries and many countries have launched their own 50/50 campaigns. WEDO has also taken the campaign to the United Nations, where it is has called on Member States to divide the top positions in their missions equally between women and men. At the end of 2002, 94 per cent of UN missions were headed by men.

number of countries in all regions. Chart 5 shows changes in women's share of seats in parliament, in the period from January 2000 to November 2002, in those countries where there have been elections (the red lines) and compares those changes to the period from 1987 to 2000 (the black lines). This may not exactly correspond to the dates of elections, since there is often a gap between the holding of elections and the posting of the results on the IPU website.

In sub-Saharan Africa, during the most recent period, there were elections in 23 countries, of which 14 increased their representation of women. Four experienced virtually no change, and four elected fewer women than previously. Mozambique and Uganda continued their upward trajectory. Equally noteworthy were the improvements in Burundi, where women's representation jumped from 6 per cent all the way to 19.5 per cent and Rwanda, where the increase was from 17.1 per cent to 25.7 per cent. However, the return to democracy in Nigeria did not result in a greater voice for women in parliament, with women's share of seats falling below its previous level of 7.3 per cent to a very disappointing 3.2 per cent. In several countries in the region, racked by internal conflicts, there is no functioning parliament.

In Northern Africa, Egypt was the only country with an election during this period but there was virtually no change, with women's share of seats stuck at just above 2 per cent.

In Central and Western Asia six countries held elections in this period, with five of them showing improvements. The increase in Tajikistan was particularly marked: Women's share went from 2.8 per cent to 12 per cent. However, Azerbaijan, which had been one of the better performers in a region where representation is on the whole not high, slipped back from 12 per cent to 10.5 per cent. In this region there are a number of countries in which women's right to stand for election, and even to vote, has not yet been recognized. These include Kuwait, Oman, Qatar, Saudi Arabia and United Arab Emirates. Oman, Qatar and Saudi Arabia have never had an elected parliament.

In Asia and the Pacific, there were elections in 16 countries, and of these nine showed some progress, three showed virtually no change and four showed deterioration. The large decline in Mongolian women's share of seats, which plummeted from 25 per cent in 1987 to 7.9 per cent in 2000, was reversed, although not dramatically. Women held 10.5 per cent of all parliamentary seats in 2002. In Bangladesh, however, women's representation was reduced from 9.1 per cent to only 2 per cent. And in Indonesia, as in Nigeria, democratization did not improve women's representation: Their share of seats fell from 11.4 per cent to 8 per cent.

Latin America and the Caribbean show significant progress in some countries, counterbalanced by deterioration in almost as many. There were elections in 16 countries during the period, during which Argentina and Costa Rica passed the 30 per cent benchmark and Nicaragua reversed its earlier decline, when it had dropped from 15 per cent in 1987 to 9.7 per cent in 2000. Women's share of seats is now at 20.7 per cent. In Mexico, although the 2000 election was heralded as a victory for democracy because it removed the Partido Revolucionario Institucional (PRI) from power after decades of unchallenged rule, there was no gain for women. Their share of seats fell slightly from 17.9 per cent to 16 per cent.

Women's share of seats in parliament has suffered dramatically in Eastern Europe during the transition to market economies. Three countries have managed to reverse that trend in recent elections: Bulgaria, where women had a 21 per cent share in 1987, dropped to 10.8 per cent in 2000, and then jumped to 26.2

per cent in 2002; Poland, which saw women's share go from 20 per cent in 1987 to 12.6 per cent in 2000 then back up to 21 per cent in 2002; and the Former Republic of Macedonia, where women's share improved from 7.5 per cent in 2000 to 17.5 per cent in 2002. In Bulgaria and Poland the increase can partly be attributed to the work of women's organizations. In Poland, OSKA, a national NGO, supported women candidates with the assistance of UNIFEM. In Bulgaria, several women's NGOs worked with a new political party to bring women into office (see Box 8).

In Russia, there is no real sign of recovery. There has been a slight change in the last two years, with women representing 5.6 per cent of parliamentarians in 2000 and 6.4 per cent in 2002, compared to their 32 per cent in 1987. In some of the new countries in the region, such as Croatia, the Czech Republic, Moldova and Slovenia, women's share of seats has increased in the last two years. At the same time, women's share fell substantially in Bosnia and Herzegovina (from a high of 21% all the way down to 6.4%), Lithuania (from 17.5 to 10.6%) and slightly less so in Ukraine (from 2.8 to 5.1%). There is clearly no guarantee that upward trajectories can be maintained or that losses can be recouped.

In Western Europe and Other Developed Countries, there were elections in 17 countries. New Zealand almost succeeded in attaining the 30 per cent goal and Australia and Spain came closer to it than ever before. However, Canada and the United Kingdom did not maintain their upward trajectory and are stuck at around 17 per cent and 24 per cent respectively. Germany and the Netherlands registered slight drops, though their shares remained above 30 per cent. The United States remained at one of the lowest levels of all developed countries: 12 per cent.

AN MDG SCORECARD

The following charts show those countries that are in the lead according to the targets and indicators set out in the Millennium Development Goals as well as those that have the furthest to go. We are presenting these charts in full recognition that many of the countries in the lead have benefited from years of development, stable political situations and robust economies (see Table 8, p. 48). That is why it is particularly noteworthy that Argentina, Costa Rica and South Africa are in this group, since none of the three have had the same social, economic or political stability as the Western Developed nations on the list.

Table 9 (p. 48) summarises the MDG indicators for those countries that have the furthest to go in achieving the goals. These are largely poor countries, many of which have suffered from internal conflict as well as other factors that intervene in their ability to attain the goals. All but one of the countries with the lowest levels of achieve- [CONTINUED ON PAGE 49]

BOX 8: WOMEN'S REPRESENTATION IN THE NEW BULGARIAN PARLIAMENT

The rise in the representation of women in Bulgaria's parliament has been credited to two factors: campaigning by women's NGOs and the policies of a new political party.

Campaigning by NGOs

- The Bulgarian Gender Research Foundation (BGRF) produced a report at the end of 2000 entitled 'Equal rights and equal opportunities for women in political life in Bulgaria,' which advocated for increased attention by political parties to the problems of women in politics and for new legislation introducing affirmative action. The report called for at least 40 per cent of the candidates in eligible positions to be women.
- The Women's Alliance for Development (WAD) conducted a pre-election campaign for more women in parliament.
- Under the slogan 'Women can do it,' the Gender Project of the Bulgaria Foundation conducted extensive training for women who wished to develop political careers.
- Women's NGOs organized meetings with parliamentarians from all the political parties and suggested changes in the electoral law that would provide for 50/50 participation of women and men in all eligible electoral positions.
- The NGOs were supported by the Gender Task Force of the Stability Pact for South Eastern Europe.

Policies of a New Political Party

In April 2001 Simeon Kobourg Gottha, the returning former King of Bulgaria, formed a new political party. The new party accepted the ideas put forward by the women's NGOs and placed women in 40 per cent of eligible positions. It went on to win the national elections in June 2001 with 40 per cent of the votes. Women won 26.2 per cent of the seats in the new parliament.

Assessment

The representation of women in the Bulgarian parliament has not been an unmitigated success. A study for the BGRF found that women in parliament were not fully prepared for their new careers. They did not see themselves as representing women's interests, nor did they see themselves as having common interests with each other. NGOs will need to continue to work with the new women parliamentarians to bring women's issues higher up on their agendas.

Source: personal communication, Genoveva Tisheva (BGRF)

Table 8: Countries with Highest Levels of Achievement in Gender Equality and Women's Empowerment

Country	30% Women's Share of Seats in National Parliament	Female/Male Ratio Net Secondary School Enrolment, (95-105%)	Female Enrolment Rate in Secondary School	Female Share of Paid Employment in Non-Agricultural Sector, (44-55%)
Sweden	45.0	104	98	51
Denmark	38.0	103	91	49
Finland	36.5	102	96	50
Norway	36.4	101	96	48
Iceland	34.9	104	78	52
Netherlands	31.5	100	92	44
Germany	31.0	101	88	45
Very Close to the Highest Levels of Achievement in Gender Equality and Women's Empowerment				
Costa Rica	35.1	113	46	39
Argentina	31.3	109	79	43
South Africa	30.0	110	95	n.d

Table 9: Countries with Lowest Levels of Achievement in Gender Equality and Women's Empowerment

Female Enrolment Rate in Secondary School	Female/Male Ratio in Secondary School Enrolment	Female Youth Literacy Rate	Female Share of Wage Employment in Non-Agricultural Sector	Women's Share of Seats in National Parliament
Below 10%	Below 50%	Below 50%	Below 20%	Below 5%
Burkina Faso	Benin	Bangladesh	Bahrain	Algeria / Morocco
Burundi	Cambodia	Benin	Burkina Faso	Armenia / Nigeria
Cambodia	Chad	Burkina Faso	Chad	Bangladesh / Niger
Chad	Côte d'Ivoire	Guinea-Bissau	India	Djibouti / Sri Lanka
Congo, DR	Equatorial Guinea	Iraq	Malawi	Egypt / Samoa (Western)
Guinea	Guinea	Mauritania	Niger	Iran / Turkey
Mozambique	Guinea-Bissau	Nepal	Pakistan	Jordan / Togo
Niger	Mali	Niger	Syria	Kenya / Yemen
Tanzania, UR	Togo	Pakistan	Turkey	Kuwait / UAE
	Yemen	Senegal	Zimbabwe	Lebanon / Vanuatu
				Mauritania

Table 10: Poverty and Economic Growth, by Region

	Percentage Population Below $1 a Day 1999	Per Capita GDP 2000 (ppp US$)	Growth of Per Capita GDP, Annual Average 1990-2000 (%)
Sub-Saharan Africa	47	1690	-0.3
Middle East and North Africa	2	4793	0.7
South Asia	37	2404	3.3
East Asia and the Pacific	14	4290	5.7
Latin America and Caribbean	15	7234	1.7
Central and Eastern Europe and Central Asia	4	6930	-2.4

Sources: Population below $1 a day: MDG data base
Per capita GDP: UNDP, *Human Development Report 2002*, Table 1, p.152
Growth of per capita GDP: *Human Development Report 2002*, Table 12, p. 193

Table 11: Maternal Mortality, by Region

	Maternal Deaths per 100,000 Live Births, 1995
Sub-Saharan Africa	1100
Middle East and North Africa	360
South Asia	430
East Asia and the Pacific	140
Latin America and Caribbean	190
CIS/CEE and Baltic States	55

Source: Maternal mortality in 1995: Estimates developed by WHO, UNICEF and UNFPA, Geneva, 2001.

[CONTINUED FROM PAGE 47] ment in girls' enrolment in secondary school and gender equality in enrolment are in sub-Saharan Africa. As numerous studies, including our own, have shown, women in this region are more disadvantaged than in any other region. As Table 10 shows, sub-Saharan Africa has the highest poverty rates and the lowest per capita GDP. Moreover, on average, the region's production is not growing but shrinking, with GDP per capita declining in the period 1990 to 2000 at an average rate of -0.3 per cent a year.

This deepening poverty has profound impacts on women's lives. As Table 11 shows, maternal mortality rates are much higher than in other regions—more than twice as high as in South Asia, the next highest region. HIV/AIDS prevalence among adults is also much higher in sub-Saharan Africa (see Table 12, p. 50)—more than four times the rates in the Caribbean which has the next highest rates.

Despite the dire conditions in sub-Saharan Africa, women are taking steps to increase their voice in public decision-making. As shown in chart 5, in most of the 23 countries in which there have been elections in the region between January 2000 and November 2002, women's share of seats in parliament has increased. At the end of 2002 women in 13 sub-Saharan countries had a higher share of seats in parliament than did women in the United States.

Women parliamentarians in several sub-Saharan countries are working together with women researchers and community activists to develop gender budget initiatives (see Box 9, p. 51). These initiatives examine the impact on gender equality of the ways in which governments raise revenue and spend money. They advocate for more attention to the priorities of poor women and greater accountability towards them, providing a beacon of hope in an area of mounting distress.

RECOMMENDATIONS

In assessing the progress of women in the context of the MDGs, the limitations of the MDG indicators become apparent. We have proposed certain alterations or additions that will provide a clearer picture of actual achievement.

1. For girls' enrolment rates in school:
- Monitor the actual level of girls' enrolment in addition to gender disparities.
- Track completion rates as well as enrolment rates.

2. For literacy:
- Track the actual level of literacy, as well as the gender disparity.

3. For women's economic equality and empowerment, develop additional indicators to:
- Track women's participation in informal wage work.
- Develop a decent work indicator.
- Create a target to end gender disparity in wages.
- Measure the extent to which women are paid a living wage.

Table 12: HIV/AIDS, by Region, 2002

	Adults and Children Living with HIV/AIDS	Adults and Children Newly Infected with HIV/AIDS	Adult Prevalence Rate (%)*	% of HIV Positive Adults Who Are Women
Sub-Saharan Africa	29.4 million	3.5 million	8.8	58
North Africa and the Middle East	550 000	83 000	0.3	55
South and South-East Asia	6.0 million	700 000	0.6	36
East Asia and the Pacific	1.2 million	270 000	0.1	24
Latin America	1.5 million	150 000	0.6	30
Caribbean	440 000	60 000	2.4	50
Eastern Europe and Central Asia	1.2 million	250 000	0.6	27
Western Europe	570 000	30 000	0.3	25
North America	980 000	45 000	0.6	20
Australia and New Zealand	15 000	500	0.1	7
Total	42 million	5 million	1.2	50

Source: UNAIDS/WHO. AIDS Epidemic Update: December 2002. http://www.unaids.org/
* The proportion of adults (15 to 49 years of age) living with HIV/AIDS in 2002, using 2002 population numbers

BOX 9: GENDER BUDGET INITIATIVES

Following the pioneering work of South Africa, at least 10 other countries in sub-Saharan Africa are carrying out gender budget initiatives, including Botswana, Malawi, Mozambique, Namibia, Nigeria, Rwanda, Senegal, Tanzania, Uganda and Zimbabwe. Started in response to the structural adjustment policies imposed in the region in the last two decades, they have highlighted the fact that the contributions of men and women to economies are counted and recompensed very differently. Women contribute 90 per cent of all food processing, water and fuelwood collection, 90 per cent of hoeing and weeding on farms and 60 per cent of harvesting and marketing, along with almost all the work of caring for family members, but most of this is unpaid.

Most of the gender budget initiatives also reflect the movement towards more transparent and participatory forms of governance in the region, including a concern to give poor and marginalized populations a political voice as well as a greater share in public resources. While parliaments are finding ways to play a greater role in determining budget priorities, women's groups and civil society organizations are advocating with parliamentarians to influence this process and providing their own analysis of existing budget flows.

As a result, some of the most effective initiatives are carried out jointly by civil society and parliamentarians. One example is the Gender Budget Project in Uganda, which is a creative partnership between the Forum for Women in Democracy (FOWODE) and a caucus of parliamentarians representing women, youth, workers and people with disabilities. Through the partnership, supported by the UN Development Programme (UNDP), UNIFEM and other international agencies, research and analyses done by FOWODE are taken up in parliamentary committees and included in parliamentary reports on the budget. Focused on expenditures in education, health and agriculture, the project has succeeded in involving government planners from those three sectors as well as the Ministries of Finance and Economic Planning and Gender, Labour and Social Development. Recently, it has also begun to focus on how revenue is raised.

Elsewhere, Tanzania's Gender Budgeting Initiative, started in 1997 by a coalition of women's groups, and taken forward by the Tanzania Gender Networking Programme, was a response to the dramatic cuts in social services, particularly to health care and education, together with massive layoffs of public sector workers caused by structural adjustment policies. In addition to examining resource allocation in national and local budgets, the initiative seeks to strengthen women's lobbying and advocacy skills in order to increase resources to sectors that impact women, youths and other disadvantaged groups. An integral part of the initiative is a popular education effort, featuring a reader-friendly guide to the budget process and economic policy.

Mozambique is an example of a government-led initiative. Under the leadership of the Ministry of Planning and Finance, the Government presented a Social and Economic Plan with a gender perspective to Parliament in 1998 and began collecting gender-disaggregated data for the 1999 budget proposals. The Ministry also facilitated training for technical staff in preparing the national budget from a gender perspective. UNIFEM has recently supported the production of a popular guidebook on gender budget analysis that aims to make women's unpaid work visible and to see that it is accounted for in macroeconomic policy making.

In Nigeria a UNIFEM-supported gender budget exercise is being developed under the leadership of the Ministry of Women's Affairs and Social Development as part of its work to implement the Beijing Platform for Action. The initiative focused first on the federal budget for agricultural and rural development as well as on two state-level budgets — the budget for health in Akwa Ibom state and the budget for commerce and industry in Ebugu state. A training manual is in the process of development. UNIFEM is also liaising with the European Union and the Open Society Institute for West Africa (OSIWA) to promote gender mainstreaming in their public budget reform programmes.

In Rwanda, which is struggling to recover from a decade of war and upheaval, the Government faces the twin challenges of building democratic governance and restarting a devastated economy. Poverty rates, especially among women, are among the highest in the region: 62 per cent of female-headed households are living in poverty compared to 54 per cent of male-headed households. Most people depend upon farming for livelihoods, but while women make up over 80 per cent of farmers, they have limited access to or control over land, markets and credit. With support from the UK Department for International Development (DfID), the Rwanda Government is carrying out a gender budget exercise under the leadership of the Ministry of Gender and Women in Development. It is collaborating with the Ministry of Finance and Economic Planning, which is coordinating reform of governance and development strategy. Starting with pilots in five sectors, the initiative is focused on building capacity within the ministries and working with the Directorate of Statistics to generate sex-disaggregated data.

Sources: Budlender et al. 2002; UNIFEM 2002

BOX 10: THE MILLENNIUM PROJECT

To accelerate progress towards achieving the Millennium Development Goals, the UN Secretary-General and the Administrator of UNDP have launched the Millennium Project, a three-year effort to identify the best strategies for meeting the MDGs. The Project's analytical work will be carried out by 10 Task Forces, comprised of representatives of academia, the public and private sectors, and civil society organizations.

The Task Force on Education and Gender Equality has produced background papers on each of its two components. The paper on gender equality, entitled "Promises to Keep: Achieving Gender Equality and the Empowerment of Women," offers an analysis of the selected targets and indicators for Goal 3, summarizes progress to date along these measures, and makes recommendations for tracking progress in the future. Many of the Task Force's observations and recommendations affirm what is contained in this volume. They also propose alternative targets and indicators for tracking progress.

The Task Force puts forward three primary domains or components of equality between men and women:

- **The capabilities domain** refers to basic human abilities as measured through education, health and nutrition. It is the most fundamental of the three domains and is necessary for achieving equality in the other two domains.
- **The access to resources and opportunities domain** refers primarily to equality in the opportunity to use or apply basic capabilities through access to economic assets (such as land and property) and resources (such as income and employment).
- **The agency domain** is the defining element in the concept of empowerment and refers to the ability to make choices and decisions that can alter outcomes. Gender equality in this domain can only result from an equalizing in the balance of power between women and men in the household and societal institutions.

These three domains of equality are inter-related. Progress in any one domain to the exclusion of the others is insufficient to meet the goal of gender equality. While they are inter-related, the three domains are not necessarily dependent on one another. For instance, illiterate women, who are lacking in the capabilities domain, may organize, thereby building their agency to influence their circumstances and those of their households. Not surprisingly, the women then use that agency to demand capability (better health or education) and opportunity (access to decent work). Similarly, women with capabilities (as measured by education) may have limited economic opportunities, owing to persistent gender discrimination in employment and access to resources.

The Task Force recommends using this framework to expand the number of targets necessary to reach Goal 3 and adding some indicators to the four that were originally selected. For the targets, it recommends two additional ones to be met by 2015: 1) eliminate gender inequality in access to economic assets and employment; 2) achieve a 30 per cent share of seats for women in national parliaments.

For the indicators, it recommends the following supplements:

- Completion rates in addition to enrolment rates for all levels of education;
- Region-specific economic indicators such as gender gaps in earnings in wage and self-employment, sex-disaggregated unemployment rates or occupational segregation;
- Prevalence of domestic violence in the past year – particularly focusing on physical violence experienced by women ages 15-49 at the hands of intimate partners.

The paper contains a brief discussion on policies and programmes needed to achieve the two proposed targets and the already-existing one. Some of the highlights include:

Target 1 – Eliminate gender disparity in primary and secondary education, preferably by 2005 and in all levels of education no later than 2015. On the global level, the authors recommend using the "Education for All" (EFA) framework established after the World Conference on Education for All in 1990 to set priorities and channel resources. The EFA declaration includes a commitment to "ensure access to and improve the quality of education for girls and women and to remove every obstacle that hampers their active participation." In 2002, the EFA Fast-Track Partnership was endorsed, which would channel increased development support to countries indentified as having a sound educational sector strategy.

At the regional and national levels, the authors highlight the need to address supply and demand constraints. On the supply side, strategies include increasing the number and reach of primary and secondary schools, particularly in rural areas; reducing school costs; staffing schools with female teachers; instituting policies that promote girls' attendance (such as permitting married adolescents to attend); and improving the safety of schools, the quality and gender-sensitivity of curricula, and the design of facilities. Demand-side strategies include mobilizing parent and community involvement in monitoring the quality of education, undertaking campaigns to increase awareness of the value of girls' education, and introducing broader economic policies that increase the returns to girls' education.

Target 2 – Eliminate gender inequality in access to economic assets and employment by the year 2015. The authors recommend using the ILO's Decent Work campaign (see Box 6, p. 38) as the global framework for mon-

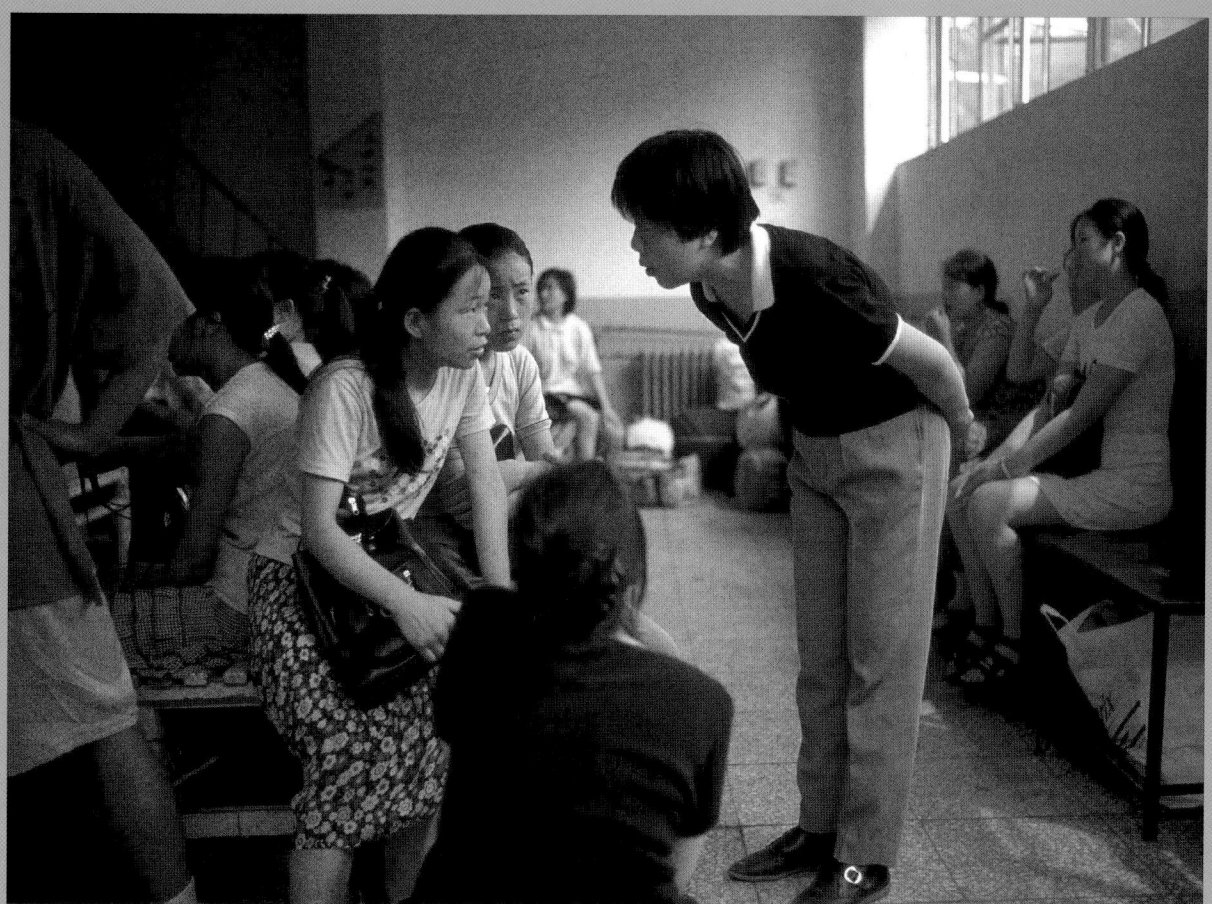

A labour market for women in Beijing. Women gather here to wait for an employer to offer them a job.

itoring equal access to employment and remedying inequalities in access to economic resources. Specifically, they propose two pathways: improving women's access to economic assets and improving women's access to employment and labour markets.

With regard to the first, they propose that an essential first step is legislation allowing women to inherit, acquire and control productive assets, including land and housing. These legal reforms will need, as well, effective enforcement mechanisms. Beyond land and housing, providing poor women with access to credit is another way to enhance their asset ownership and access to savings. Microcredit programmes have been recognized as contributing to the stabilization of household income, although they are less effective in stimulating economic growth. With regard to employment and labour markets, the authors note that strategies for improving women's access to employment include expanding their advancement from primary to tertiary schooling and boosting their participation in science, engineering, technology and other fields to prepare them for jobs in the global economy. They also note the importance of: a) employment-targeted economic growth as a prerequisite for low-income countries coupled with social policies that eliminate discriminatory employment barriers; b) equity in earnings, with secure earnings as an important means to Simprove women's bargaining power; c) equitable distribution of state resources that close gender gaps in economic and social well-being.

Target 3 – Achieve a 30 per cent share of seats for women in national parliaments by the year 2015. The authors point out that quotas have been an effective way of bringing about change in the number of women in positions of political leadership in the short term. While noting that opinion is mixed about whether or not a greater number of women in political office translates into policies and budget authorizations that benefit women overall, they point out that it does have an important symbolic effect by generating a public discussion of gender equality in politics and decision-making.

In addition to the discussion of the targets and indicators, the authors propose that women's agency can be increased by a commitment to ending violence against women. They call on the Secretary-General of the UN to lend his leadership to a campaign of zero tolerance for such violence, and recommend CEDAW as a useful international mechanism to hold countries accountable for meeting Goal 3. They point out that all the nations that have ratified CEDAW are required to report on the specific measures they have taken to advance women's status, and that the CEDAW mechanism can similarly be used to monitor progress toward the MDGs.

Source: Grown et al. 2003

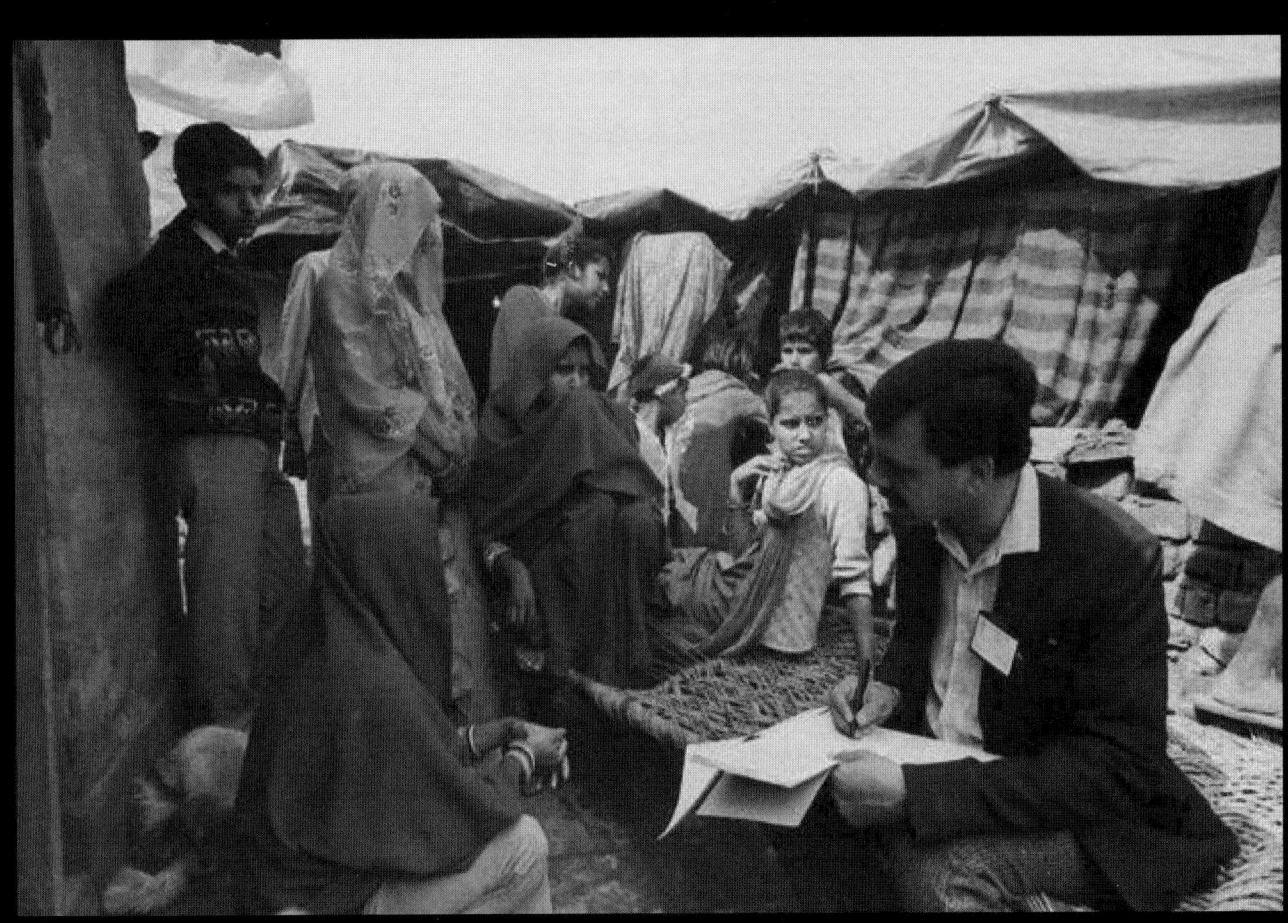
A census taker interviews a woman in an Indian village.

SECTION II

GENDER EQUALITY AND THE MILLENNIUM DEVELOPMENT GOALS

innovations in measuring and monitoring

The achievement of the MDGs will require broad social mobilization, including not only governments and development agencies but also civil society. Women's organizations will need to be vigilant in international and national monitoring of achievements. National level monitoring will be particularly important in assessing progress towards the achievement of Goal 3 and the gender dimensions of all other goals. As we have shown in this report, the selected MDG indicators for Goal 3 do not address many of the dimensions of women's disadvantage and are not equally relevant to all countries. Thus, the values of the Millennium Declaration will need to be translated into additional country-specific targets and indicators related to the women of that country. Numerous UN agencies have been providing support to countries to identify, construct and use such indicators. UNIFEM, for instance, has worked to strengthen the capacity of national statistical offices and of women's organizations to help them use indicators to monitor the fulfilment of commitments and to bring about positive change.

One challenge is to 'liberate' data from the files of national statistical offices. Most national statistical offices have much more data than they make public. As Patricia Alexander, Regional Adviser on Poverty and Statistics for the UN Economic and Social Commission for Asia and the Pacific (ESCAP) has noted, "Now that we are in the computer age, not only is data gathered on forms that record the sex of every respondent, any educated researcher can use these data to link the 'sex' variable to any element in the survey.

Our struggle now is to let advocates know that the data really are there—and to convince governments to make the data available."

Another challenge is to train more people to be effective users of gender-sensitive indicators in policy advocacy and in monitoring commitments. As Ela Bhatt, the activist and founder of the Self-Employed Women's Association (SEWA) in India, has said 'Statistics in the hands of activists have power.' UNIFEM is working with ESCAP to build this capacity in a number of Asian countries by developing teams of trainers for each country. Each team will consist of an economist, a statistician from the national statistical office and a gender specialist who will participate in workshops geared to helping them identify issues relevant to women in their country. They will use hands-on exercises based on data they have collected for their country, and then work within their country to build skills in the use of indicators and statistics among national women's machineries, women's NGOs and local community groups. Ultimately, however, greater capacity requires greater resources, which is the responsibility of the entire international community, especially the wealthy nations.

IMPROVING NATIONAL STATISTICS

There are many ways to use statistics to construct indicators of progress. But first the statistics must be collected and made available. UNIFEM has for many years supported initiatives to improve the availability of sex-disaggregated statistics at the country and regional level. At the country level, the basis for all national statistics is the census. While in theory this registers the activities of each individual, the way it is carried out in many cases makes women's activities less visible than men's. Many women are not considered part of the 'economically active' population if they work in the household or the fields. Women may also be asked to name their primary or secondary occupation, rather than to indicate the kind of work that they do to support their families. In many cases, women are not even interviewed; instead, the so-called head of household, usually a man, is asked to describe the work of everyone in the family. The end result is a database that is inherently flawed, compounded by the fact that countries typically do not compile and tabulate all relevant data on a sex-disaggregated basis.

To create a better model, UNIFEM, along with other international agencies, has been supporting projects to 'engender' census-taking. In the 2001 census in Nepal and India, it supported training for census takers on ways to probe for gender-sensitive information and aided the Census Bureau's work to provide sex-disaggregated results and to come up with statistical tables addressing gender issues. The ultimate goal is to ensure that these gender-sensitive methods are institutionalized in the collection and analysis of data from here on. In the Arab States UNIFEM has initiated a project entitled Gender Equality Measured through Statistics (GEMS) in June 2002. This focuses on building gender statistics relating to decision making, the formal and informal economy and violence against women. It will also mainstream gender into the structures of the national Departments of Statistics in Egypt, Jordan, and Syria.

The statistical system being set up in newly independent East Timor will have a gender perspective built in right from the start, thanks to assistance from UNIFEM and the ESCAP Statistics Division. This is probably the first time anywhere in the world that gender has been built in at the time a national statistical system was created.

Once produced, sex-disaggregated statistics need to be made available in easy to use forms. Following the publication of *Progress of the World's Women 2000*, UNIFEM assisted in the production of a number of regional and country level statistical reports: *Progress of South Asian Women 2000; Women in Mongolia: Mapping Progress under Transition;* and *Status of Nigerian Women and Men 2000: A Statistical Profile*. In addition, *Progress of Brazilian Women* will be published in 2003 with support from the Ford Foundation, and the UNIFEM regional office in the Caribbean will be publishing a new report entitled *Monitoring the Progress of Caribbean Women: Beijing + 5 and Beyond*.

Experiments are also being conducted on providing information about statistics that may be more accessible. In the Philippines, Bobbie Ericta, Head of the Philippines National Statistical Office, runs a radio programme, in which she includes segments on gender-based statistics. She reports a strong following for the programme, particularly among women, even though it airs at six in the morning. In Brazil, a CD ROM, 'The Condition of Women in Brazilian Society: Labour and Education,' was produced by the Instituto Brasileiro de Administração Municipal (IBAM), with the support of the German Cooperation Agency (GTZ), the European Commission and UNIFEM. The CD, which maps out the situation in more than 5,000 municipalities, has been distributed to 509 municipalities in Brazil, and to national, state and municipal official women's machineries. Similar exercises are being carried out in Argentina, Paraguay and Uruguay.

CREATING ALTERNATIVE INDICATORS AND INDICES

Once indicators are available, they need to be put to use, documenting progress — or the lack of it — in improving women's lives. Many initiatives are under way in this area, through international,

Table 13: Index of Fulfilled Commitments

Countries	Thematic Areas	Citizen Participation and Access to Power	Economic Autonomy and Employment	Women's Health and Reproductive Rights	Overall
Chile	1995	20.78	80.71	66.63	61.87
	1998	25.00	75.18	69.12	61.64
Ecuador	1995	9.37	75.39	49.49	49.98
	1998	15.78	73.32	48.68	50.38
Paraguay	1995	11.27	72.70	58.20	52.37
	1998	35.65	69.52	67.77	60.36
Uruguay	1995	8.13	71.20	21.29	38.15
	1998	13.94	72.19	44.66	49.72

Source: Facultad Latinoamericana de Ciencias Sociales (FLACSO) 2003, *Index of Fulfilled Commitments* (forthcoming), Santiago, Chile

regional and national agencies as well as through civil society groups that create and monitor their own indicators.

CIVIL SOCIETY INITIATIVES

Civil society groups are creating indicators that can be used not only to enhance the picture provided by government statistics but also to prod governments to meet their commitments to women.

Women's organizations in many countries in Latin America are working to construct measures of how far their governments have fulfilled the commitments they have made to women. With technical support from FLACSO (Facultad Latinoamericana de Ciencias Sociales), and financial support from UNIFEM, Indices of Fulfilled Commitments have been constructed in Chile, Ecuador, Paraguay and Uruguay. Work on an Index is proceeding in Argentina, Colombia and Peru and is in the planning stages in Bolivia, Dominican Republic, Guatemala, Honduras, Mexico, Panama and Venezuela.

Three thematic areas have been chosen for each country's index:
- Citizen participation and access to power
- Economic autonomy and employment
- Women's health and reproductive rights

Within each theme, the commitments made by governments at UN conferences and in their national plans of action relating to women are translated into quantitative targets, and indicators of progress towards them are identified. The degree of fulfillment of each target is measured. Then the women involved in the initiative agree on how to weight the individual components to create an index for the percentage of the target achieved in recent years for each thematic area as well as for the three themes combined. (For more details of the methods used to produce the figures, see FLACSO, 2001; 2003). The strength of this method is that it reflects the priorities of women's organizations in each country: They decide which commitments to prioritize, how to translate these into targets and how to measure progress towards the targets.

Results for Chile, Ecuador, Paraguay and Uruguay are shown in Table 13. Care must be taken in interpreting this data because the women in each country may have made different choices about how to construct their index. However, we can conclude from the table that in 1998 none of the four governments had yet fulfilled all the commitments of greatest priority to the women in those countries. The Governments of Chile and Paraguay were doing better than those of Ecuador and Uruguay in fulfilling their commitments. In all four countries fulfillment of commitments in relation to citizen participation and access to power was lowest, and it was highest in relation to economic autonomy and employment.

Women are now beginning to use the Indices of Fulfilled Commitments to lobby for change. In Chile, the Grupo Iniciativa Mujeres brought the results of their work to the attention of women leaders, presented them to women in parliament and discussed them with ministers and officials. They also mounted a publicity campaign in the press. Their message was that progress was too slow overall and that at current rates, it would be 2036 before all the goals were achieved. As a result of their efforts some changes were made in programmes for women:
- Quotas were introduced to increase the amount of credit per capita given by the government to rural women.
- Quotas were introduced to increase the number of women receiving tax-exempt skills-training.
- Legal changes were made to allow voluntary sterilization at women's request.
- Legal changes were made to allow vasectomy to be used as a sterilization method.

Teresa Valdés, FLACSO coordinator of the effort, points out that women now see the impor-

Table 14: Changes in Gender Gaps, 1990-2000

	Illiteracy (15-24 Years)	Unemployment	Primary School Enrolment (Gross)
No. of Countries	87	133	163
Deterioration	13.5%	30.3%	20.7%
Improvement	38.3%	43.8%	32.9%

Adapted from Social Watch 2002

tance of statistics for political activism: "Women tell me that statistics can be really interesting. Our experience shows that indicators really can help to bring about change for women."

Social Watch is another civil society group in Latin America that has been producing innovative indicators to monitor women's progress. Based at the Instituto del Tercer Mundo in Uruguay, and building on an international network of citizens' groups in over 40 countries, Social Watch has for several years been producing reports on social progress, including women's, charting life expectancy, reduction in illiteracy and net enrolment of girls in primary school. In 2002 a new chart was introduced focusing on gender gaps rather than absolute levels of women's capacities and opportunities. The indicators chosen were the female to male ratio in youth illiteracy rates, unemployment rates and primary school enrolment rates. The choice does not appear to have been directly linked to monitoring the MDGs. Social Watch provides a country by country chart and also a global summary table, the results of which are shown in Table 14.

The table shows that, in the case of illiteracy, for example, 38.3 per cent of the 87 countries for which data was available experienced a reduction in the gender gap, meaning that women approached parity with men, while the gap increased in 13.5 per cent of countries. In all three areas, the gender gap has decreased in more countries than it has increased. Unfortunately there is no discussion of the extent to which the narrowing of gaps represents a true improvement of women's situation or merely an equalizing of deprivation. In the case of illiteracy, for example, it is difficult to compare the figures compiled in this report with Social Watch's figures to see if women's situation has improved, because Social Watch tracks illiteracy and we track literacy. However, a deterioration in the gender gap for illiteracy can be consistent with young women becoming more literate worldwide, as indicated in our work.

Social Watch has a number of other indicators that are important for monitoring progress for women. In particular, it provides indicators of progress or regression in access to the basic public services that are so important in lightening the burden of unpaid care work:

- percentage of population with access to health services
- number of pregnancies attended by trained health personnel (per 1,000 live births)
- percentage of deliveries attended by trained health personnel
- percentage of population with access to sanitation
- percentage of population with access to safe water

NEW REGIONAL AND NATIONAL INDICATORS AND INDICES

There are several important ongoing efforts to create new databases in various regions. In Africa, the UN Economic Commission for Africa is planning a new set of indicators, the Gender Status Index and an African Women's Progress Scoreboard, both of which will be published in the *African Women's Report* in 2003. These will contain data collected directly from the national statistical offices of African countries, and will thus be able to make use of a wider range of data than is generally supplied by UN agencies. The Gender Status Index will combine about 20 indicators of gender gaps in social, economic and political power, giving each equal weighting, and thus implicitly judging that all of the gender gaps measured are of equal importance. In this respect the Index is different from the Indices of Fulfilled Commitments being developed in Latin America, which give different weighting to the components of each Index according to priorities agreed upon by various civil society groups.

The African Gender Status Index is also different in that it does not refer to the achievement of particular goals. Instead, it will have some similarities to the Gender Sensitive Human Development Index in the Human Development Reports. Like those, its usefulness will come from comparing African countries both at one point in time and over time. As measured by the Index, the country with the highest score will be the one with the greatest gender equality. If the score on the Index rises, it will signal an increase in gender equality. However, it will not be possible to see what factors are responsible for high and low scores, nor the

CHART 6: Distribution of Total Hours Worked in Cuba, by Sex, 2001

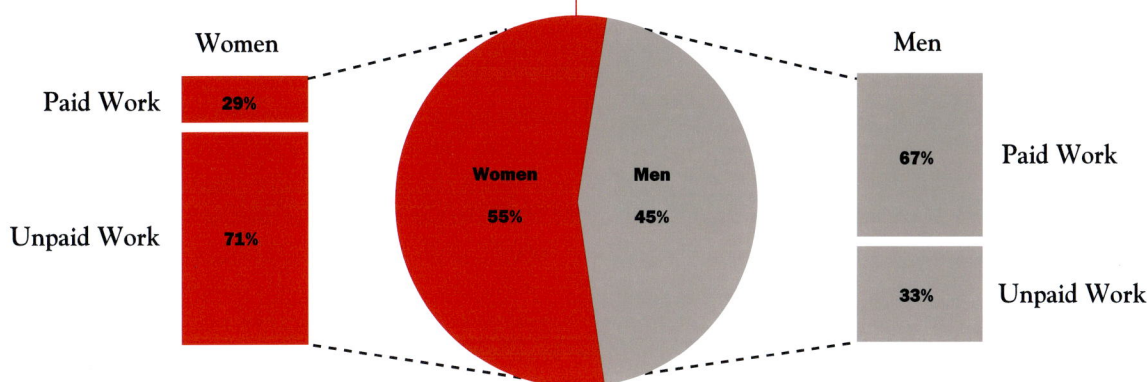

Adapted from Teresa Lara Junco, General Coordinator of the Cuban Time-Use Survey

extent to which the scores represent equality in deprivation or equality in prosperity, unless the underlying tables of indicators are also published. The scoreboard, which will monitor progress towards improvements in law, policies and budget allocations, will be constructed with input from NGOs.

There are many other examples of government offices helping to create new indicators that will broaden their knowledge of women's status. UNDP, UNFPA, UNICEF and UNIFEM recently signed a memorandum of understanding with the Kenyan Government to support the creation and dissemination of data and statistical information for development. In Central America and Mexico UNIFEM has supported the creation of a national statistical system (SISESIM) that monitors the implementation of national programmes for equal opportunities and the advancement of women. In Mexico the SISESIM data comparing school drop-out rates and completion of studies by boys and girls showed that girls were dropping out at a higher rate than boys. It led to the recognition that poor families needed extra assistance to keep girls in school. As a result PROGRESA, a government anti-poverty programme, now provides larger schooling grants for girls than for boys.

UNIFEM has also been championing time use surveys as a means of collecting expanded data about women's work. Time use, unlike share of employment, gives a more complete picture of women's work, whether in the home or outside it. The Cuban statistical office, with support from UNIFEM, as part of a larger UNDP project funded by the Italian government, conducted its first national time use survey in 2001. The results are presented in Chart 6. They show that women spend less time than men on paid work and more time than men on unpaid work. But when women's total hours of paid and unpaid work are added up, they spend many more hours working than men do.

Another region where time use studies are relevant is sub-Saharan Africa, where they can reveal some of the hidden costs of HIV/AIDS. UNIFEM, in collaboration with the Tropical Institute of Community Health and Development (TICH) in Kenya, has just concluded the first phase of a multi-country participatory research project on the gender dimensions of HIV/AIDS care policies and practices in Djibouti, Ethiopia, Kenya and Somalia. The study established that women carry the heavier burden of both unpaid and paid care (UNIFEM/TICH 2002).

Also in East Africa UNIFEM is sponsoring innovative district level surveys such as the 'gender and household food economy assessment' that was conducted in the Hiran region of Somalia. The survey collected sex-disaggregated data from households on income, priority expenditures, coping strategies and access to and control over resources. It showed that although women are the main actors in production and marketing, they do not have full control over their income. Indeed, about 10 per cent of their income goes towards their male partners' daily allowance for khat (an addictive substance used in many parts of the Horn of Africa). The study contributed to advocacy work within the Food Security Network for Somalia, which began targeting women in food security and livelihood programmes. The Network has also decided to use the survey as a prototype for its future work. The findings have also been used to inform the modified UN Joint Action Recovery Programme for Somalia.

Statistics are also an important part of the effort to end violence against women. They provide essen-

Table 15: Gender and Poverty in Latin America

Country	Area	Proportion Below Poverty Line M=male F=female	Females per 100 Males Below Poverty Line
Argentina	Urban	23.8 (M) 23.6 (F)	99.3
Bolivia	Urban	48.6 (M) 48.2 (F)	101.4
	Rural	79.4 (M) 81.6 (F)	102.8
Brazil	Urban	33.0 (M) 32.6 (F)	99.5
	Rural	54.8 (M) 55.6 (F)	101.6
Chile	Urban	20.6 (M) 20.6 (F)	101.0
	Rural	26.4 (M) 28.8 (F)	109.1
Colombia	Urban	48.5 (M) 48.1 (F)	100.4
	Rural	57.5 (M) 60.7 (F)	105.8
Costa Rica	Urban	16.8 (M) 19.2 (F)	114.4
	Rural	20.8 (M) 23.8 (F)	114.5
Ecuador	Urban	63.1 (M) 63.3 (F)	102.8
El Salvador	Urban	38.1 (M) 39.0 (F)	101.3
	Rural	64.9 (M) 65.4 (F)	100.8
Guatemala	Urban	45.7 (M) 45.4 (F)	101.0
	Rural	69.8 (M) 70.0 (F)	100.4
Honduras	Urban	66.6 (M) 65.4 (F)	99.3
	Rural	81.0 (M) 81.5 (F)	100.8
Mexico	Urban	38.7 (M) 38.7 (F)	101.0
	Rural	58.3 (M) 58.6 (F)	100.6
Nicaragua	Urban	63.4 (M) 64.5 (F)	101.7
	Rural	77.4 (M) 76.6 (F)	99.0
Panama	Urban	25.8 (M) 26.6 (F)	103.1
	Rural	40.4 (M) 43.6 (F)	107.9
Paraguay	Urban	49.7 (M) 47.4 (F)	97.1
	Rural	73.2 (M) 74.4 (F)	101.9
Dominican Republic	Urban	33.9 (M) 36.9 (F)	110.2
	Rural	37.7 (M) 43.3 (F)	115.0
Uruguay	Urban	9.7 (M) 9.4 (F)	97.3
Venezuela	Total	48.6 (M) 50.0 (F)	104.3

Source: ECLAC, *Demographic Bulletin*, July 2002, Tables 6a and 6b

tial information on incidence as well as which types of interventions work best. There are several important research projects going on that will develop useful statistical information on violence against women. The World Bank, the Inter-American Development Bank, the Centre for Research on Violence Against Women and Children in Canada, and the UK-based Centre for Health and Gender Equity (CHANGE) are all conducting studies to estimate the personal, social and economic costs of violence against women. In addition, the European Institute for Crime Prevention and Control, the UN Interregional Crime and Justice Research Institute and Statistics Canada are coordinating the International Violence Against Women Survey, which will utilize a standard questionnaire and rely largely on the network and infrastructure of the International Crime Victim Survey (ICVS) that is used in more than 70 countries around the world. The World Health Organization maintains a database on intimate partner violence and physical violence against women. It has just completed one groundbreaking study, the *World Report on Violence and Health,* and is in the midst of a multi-country study on violence against women.

ECLAC has also been a leader in developing statistical models and indicators that can be compared across regions. With support from UNIFEM, it is currently working on a Gender Statistics and Indicators model to measure the incidence and evolution of violence against women. Research will focus on women aged 15 years and older, and document various social and economic factors such as age, economic participation, family structure of the household, education level and area of residence. The hope — and expectation — is that all national institutes of statistics will participate in generating information. In the Commonwealth of Independent States, the UNIFEM regional office is supporting a nine-country survey on violence against women, covering Azerbaijan, Belarus, Kazakhstan, Kyrgyzstan, Lithuania, Moldova, Russia, Tajikistan and Uzbekistan

GENDER AND POVERTY

For Latin America and the Caribbean, ECLAC has produced a set of gender-sensitive indicators, published in the July 2002 edition of the *Demographic Bulletin*. The section on gender and income poverty is particularly noteworthy. Currently, there is no international database that allows us to monitor the extent of women's poverty, and the degree to which women are poorer than men. The MDG indicators for Goal 1, eradicating extreme poverty and hunger, are not designed in a gender-sensitive way. The ECLAC indicators are thus innovative in providing gender-sensitive information on a systematic basis for the whole region. ECLAC also goes beyond disaggregation by sex of household head to develop new indicators of the kind called for in *Progress of World's Women 2000*.

For example, in selected countries of Latin America, the indicators assess the proportions of males and females in households below the national poverty line and the number of females in households below the poverty line for every 100 males below that line. The key results are presented in Table 15. The proportion of females below the poverty line is higher than that of males in the majority of cases (taking urban and rural as separate cases). However, in about half the cases where the proportion in poverty is higher for women, men's proportion is not significantly lower.

In actual numbers, there are more poor females than poor males in the majority of cases reported, although once again, in at least half the cases the numbers of females and males living in poverty are quite close. These figures suggest that the feminization of poverty, in which a disproportionate number of females live in households below the poverty line, is present in some countries in Latin America but by no means all. It is somewhat more prevalent in rural than in urban areas. Although there is a commonly held belief that women often comprise up to 70 per cent of those living below the poverty line, this does not hold true for Latin America. If it did, there would be more than 200 females per 100 males below the poverty line. The highest figure recorded in Table 15 is 115 in rural Dominican Republic.

The World Bank has recently released an analysis of women's equality and their participation in the labour market in Latin America and the Caribbean, which has similar findings to Table 15. *Challenges and Opportunities for Gender Equality in Latin America and the Caribbean* (Ruiz Abril 2003) shows that "in spite of significant progress over the past 20 years, gender inequalities continue to be an obstacle for the full development of the countries in the region," according to María Valeria Peña, the leader of the World Bank's Gender Unit for the region.

The study shows that even though women's participation in the formal economy continues to increase, their share remains much lower than men's and they earn less than men. The situation is particularly difficult for women in rural areas, who are among the poorest and must cope with a high number of dependents, high fertility rates and lack of access to land. Landlessness in fact is on the increase in several countries, such as Chile, Colombia, Costa Rica, El Salvador, Honduras and Nicaragua according to the Bank. Mexico remains the country with the biggest gender gap in land ownership: Women represent only 21 per cent of the property owners under land reform.

Table 16: Gender and Poverty in India

Year	Location	Percentage of Poor Among Adult Males	Percentage of Poor Among Adult Females
1983	Rural	36.7	38.7
1983	Urban	31.4	34.9
1993/1994	Rural	23.5	24.9
1993/1994	Urban	26.5	29.5

Source: Banerjee, 2000, using data from the Indian national consumption expenditure surveys

Nirmala Banerjee, a researcher at the Centre for the Study of Social Sciences in India, where many of the world's poorest women live, has conducted research similar to that done by ECLAC. She has reported that in both rural and urban India, a higher proportion of the adult female population lives below the poverty line than of the adult male population. And even though there was a reduction in both male and female poverty incidence between 1983 and 1993, women remained disproportionately poor (see Table 16).

There is much about women's poverty that is not captured by such statistics. Poor women and girls who are unable to survive on their own may have to seek shelter with relatives in households living above the poverty line. They may be working as live-in servants in households that are above the poverty line. If they have little or no income of their own, or work as live-in servants, their lives may lack dignity, autonomy and security, even though they have enough to eat and adequate shelter. They may be particularly vulnerable to violence. The next goal for those developing statistics and indicators will be to develop ones that help us understand these wider dimensions of gender, poverty and violence. The Women and Development Unit at ECLAC is working on this, and among the indicators they plan to produce is one on the proportion of women with no cash income of their own.

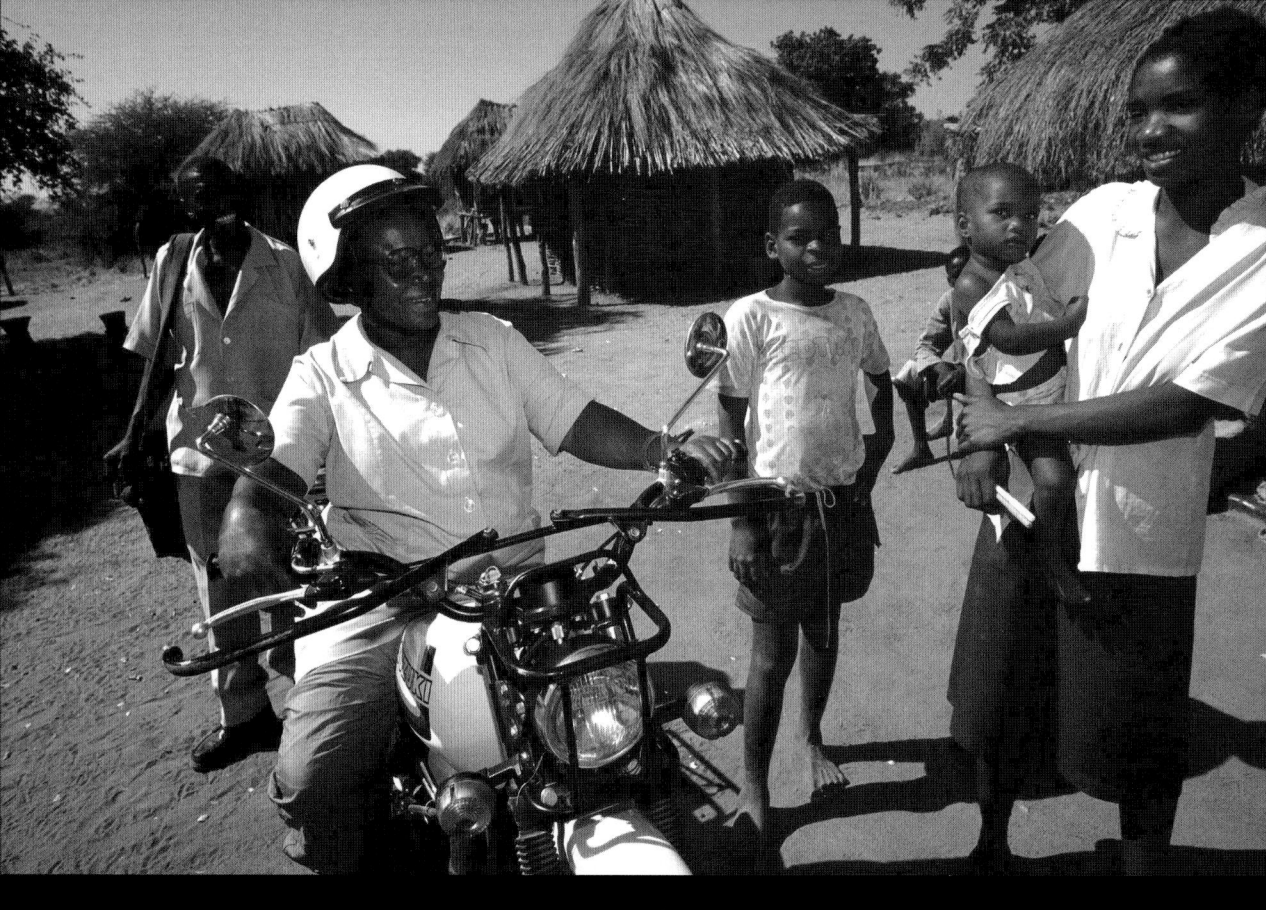
This nurse uses a motorcycle to bring health care to outlying villages in Zimbabwe.

Conclusion

GENDER EQUALITY AND THE MILLENNIUM DEVELOPMENT GOALS

moving forward

The information in these tables and charts indicates that although women have made great strides in recent years, there is still much to be done, both to move forward and to prevent falling back. At this critical time in international politics, world leaders must find a way to ensure growth, development and hope for everyone — women and men alike. Public policy for the empowerment of women has to focus on new ways of including women and enabling them to shape the institutions that structure their lives. Empowerment is essentially about the ability to make choices and exercise bargaining power; to have a voice; to have the ability to organize and influence the direction of social change; to create a just social and economic order, nationally and internationally (UNIFEM 1997).

Goal 8, which envisions a global partnership for development and which is one of the more innovative of the Millennium Development Goals, could help to assure women's empowerment. It is therefore disappointing to see no mention of women's inclusion and participation in the targets set for this goal. Many women's organizations have also pointed out this lack, and have expressed concern that the targets as specified may not promote desirable forms of development. For example, Target 12 seems to suggest that liberalization of trade and finance is beneficial — but many scholars and activists have shown that unless it is carefully managed, it makes the lives of many poor women even more insecure than they were before. Moreover, some of the targets fall short of what many advocates for social justice think is required. For example, Target 15 calls for measures to make debt sustainable, rather than the cancelation of debt. The targets implicitly assume that the key partners are governments of rich and poor countries, working in conjunction with private businesses, especially pharmaceutical and information technology companies. There is no mention of women's organizations, or indeed of any civil society organization or NGOs. The vision embedded in the targets for Goal 8 is currently that of a top-down partnership.

Women's and other civil society organizations must begin organizing now to create and present strategies for reversing this by proposing bottom-up partnerships which hold governments and corporations accountable for plans that truly create development that is beneficial to all. At the same time, advocates must continue to press forward on the many commitments made to women by the international conferences of the 1990s that are not included in the Millennium Development Goals but are central to women's empowerment. There is no one path to gender equality, but there can be no gender equality unless all the different paths and different issues are confronted. Economic empowerment without reproductive rights and health care will leave women less than full citizens. Education without an end to harassment and violence against women will make it difficult for girls and women to make full use of their education. For this reason and many more, UNIFEM has spearheaded major UN inter-agency campaigns, in particular with women's organizations and the media to end violence against women in Latin America and the Caribbean, Asia, Eastern Europe and the CIS countries and Africa.

As UNIFEM has argued elsewhere, persistent gender inequality is a human rights violation that must be addressed through a variety of remedies, many of which are contained in CEDAW. The Convention provides guidance when considering ways in which to end gender inequality and can provide useful recommendations on the most critical next steps in a wide range of areas relevant to the MDGs.

The world can no longer afford to make commitments that cannot or will not be kept. Future stability and progress itself depend upon the decisions we make now — to fulfill commitments and to ensure that the world's most desperately poor people, many of whom are women, have the guarantee of a better future.

TECHNICAL NOTES

GEOGRAPHICAL COVERAGE

Data is presented following the list of countries and their geographical area classification used by the United Nations Statistical Division in compiling *The World's Women 2000: Trends and Statistics*. In common with comparable UN and World Bank reports, this report does not include the following small countries, territories, islands and states owing to problems of data accessibility: American Samoa, Andorra, Antigua and Barbuda, Aruba, Bermuda, Dominica, French Guyana, French Dominica, Gaza Strip, Grenada, Guadeloupe, Guam, Kiribati, Liechtenstein, Macao, Marshall Islands, Martinique, Micronesia (Federal States of), Monaco, Netherlands Antilles, New Caledonia, Palau, Puerto Rico, Saint Kitts and Nevis, Saint Lucia, Saint Vincent and the Grenadines, San Marino, Sao Tome and Principe, Solomon Islands and U.S. Virgin Islands.

The designations do not imply the expression of any opinion on the part of UNIFEM concerning the legal status of any country, territory and area of its authorities, or concerning the delimitation of its frontiers or boundaries.

DATA SOURCES

Compiling an up-to-date and comprehensive set of figures has not been an easy task because of discrepancies and inconsistencies between different sources. We would particularly like to thank Jens Johansen at UNESCO, Sophia Lawrence at ILO and Emmanuel Boudard at the Human Development Report Office for their help.

The main data sources we have used are:
- MDG Database, Millennium Development Indicators and Series, http://millenniumindicators.un.org
- UNESCO Institute of Statistics, http://portal.unesco.org/uis
- International Labour Organization (ILO) Laboursta database, website http://laborsta.ilo.org
- ILO Bulletin of Labour Statistics, 2001 (no. 1-4)
- Electronic data file provided by ILO.
- Inter-Parliamentary Union (IPU), website http://www.ipu.org

GENDER EQUALITY IN EDUCATION
Secondary School Enrolment

Chart 1 shows the ratio of girls' net enrolment rate to boys' net enrolment rate. This is the measure of gender disparity in education used by the Taskforce working on MDG 3 and by the Human Development Report. The MDG database provides a different measure: the ratio of the number of girls enrolled in school to the number of boys enrolled in school. The argument for the MDG database measure of gender disparity in education is that it only requires information on school attendance and not on the population of school age. However, its disadvantage is that it deflects attention away from the issue of whether the same proportion of girls of school age are enrolled in school as are boys. This is the key issue, not the absolute numbers. A focus on enrolment rates is essential for understanding whether reductions in gender disparity are being achieved through increases in the enrolment of girls or decreases in the enrolment of boys. It is important not only to examine the gap between boys' and girls' secondary enrolment rates but also the level of enrolment of girls, the latest available data (2001) for which is shown in table 1. Due to recent changes in the UNESCO classification of levels of education, data on girls' net enrolment rates since 1997 are not compatible with the data on rates before 1997. Therefore it has not been possible to assess on a country by country basis how far there has been an improvement between 1997 and 2001. The MDG database does not provide this indicator.

We calculated the ratio of girls' net enrolment rate to boys' net enrolment rate for Chart 1 using data on net and gross enrolment rates for girls and boys from the UNESCO Institute for Statistics http://portal.unesco.org/uis.

The primary sources of enrolment data are national ministries of education, which collect the data from schools and report it to UNESCO. The reliability of data varies according to the effectiveness of record keeping in each school. Where resource allocation to schools depends upon enrolment numbers, there may be an incentive to over-report enrolment. Accurate calculations of enrolment rates also depend upon estimates of the population of school-age children, the reliability of which is variable.

Gross enrolment rates measure the number of children enrolled in primary or secondary school as a percentage of the total number of children in the relevant age group for that level. These rates can be greater than 100 per cent because many children of secondary school age may still be attending primary school, while young people who are past the normal age of completion of secondary school may still be attending secondary school if they have not yet attained the desired qualifications. Net enrolment rates show the number of children enrolled at a schooling level and belonging to the relevant age group for that level, expressed as a percentage of the total number of children in that age group. Net enrolment rates are better indicators and are used here whenever possible. Where this is not available we use the gross enrolment rate.

LITERACY

Chart 2 shows the ratio of female youth literacy rate to male youth literacy rate, 2002. 'Youth' is defined as people aged 15 to 24. Note that the MDG website refers to this indicator as "women to men parity index, as ratio of literacy rates, aged 15-24." Table 2 shows the level of female youth literacy in 2002 and Chart 3 presents the change in female youth literacy rate, 1995-2002. Data for both of the literacy indicators is taken from the MDG database.

Literacy is the capacity to use the skills of reading and writing in everyday life. The primary source of data is national governments, who in turn report the data to UNESCO. The problem is that there is no standard test of literacy and different countries measure it in different ways. In some cases it is inferred on the basis of years of schooling rather than on the basis of demonstrated skills. This means that care must be exercised in using literacy data, particularly in comparing the achievements of different countries. UNESCO is leading an international effort to improve literacy data.

Neither the MDG database nor UNESCO, which supplies the data to the database, had up-to-date information on the following countries: **sub-Saharan Africa**-Angola, Gabon, Guinea, Reunion, Seychelles, Sierra Leone, Somalia; **Central and Western Asia**-Azerbaijan, Georgia, Kazakhstan, Kyrgyzstan, Turkmenistan; **Asia and the Pacific**-Afghanistan, East Timor DR, Korea DPR, Samoa (Western), Vanuatu; **Latin America and the Caribbean**-Barbados, Suriname; **Eastern Europe**-Bosnia and Herzegovina, Czech Rep., Slovakia, Yugoslavia FR.; **Western Europe and Other Developed Countries** (with the exception of Greece, Italy, Malta, Portugal, Spain).

For Table 3: Length of Time Needed to Achieve 95% Female Youth Literacy Rate at Current Rates of Change, the calculation for Column 4-Number of Years Needed to Reach 95% Literacy Rate was performed using the following methodology:

$V = Ae^{rt}$ expressing this in natural logarithm (ln= natural logarithm):

$\ln V = \ln(Ae^{rt})$
$\ln V = \ln A + rt \ln e \quad (\ln e = 1)$
Therefore,
$\ln V = \ln A + rt$
$\ln V - \ln A = rt$
$t = \dfrac{\ln V - \ln A}{r}$

V = target rate of female youth literacy
A = present female youth literacy rate, 2002
r = average annual rate of change
t = years

(Source: Chiang, A. 1984. Fundamental Methods of Mathematical Economics. McGraw-Hill, USA)

GENDER EQUALITY IN EMPLOYMENT

Table 4 shows the latest data available on female share of wage employment in the non-agricultural sector and Chart 4 shows changes in this share comparing the early 1980s, mid 1990s and latest data available. The ILO defines wage employment as that which relates "solely to employees (wage earners and salaried employees) in employment" (ILO Labour Statistics Yearbook, 1998). Non-agricultural economic activities (industry and services) are defined according to the International Standard Industrial Classification (ISIC) and include mining and quarrying; manufacturing; electricity, gas and water; and construction and services (both private and public sector). The primary data is supplied to ILO by national governments, which collect it from a variety of sources: labour-related establishment surveys and censuses; official estimates; insurance records; labour force surveys; administrative records and related sources. This creates problems of compatibility; in some cases women's share is particularly low because of the reliance on surveys that exclude much of women's employment. A further problem is that many countries do not include all non-agricultural activities.

The MDG database does report this indicator but we found that the figures it gave were not always consistent with those in the ILO online Laboursta database. Fortunately we were able to benefit from the advice of Sophia Lawrence, statistician at the ILO, who provided us with a set of the latest unpublished data. We excluded Paraguay because data is reported for only four non-agricultural sectors: mining, manufacturing, construction, and transport. We found that this data file was not comprehensive and we have supplemented it with data from ILO's *Bulletin of Labour Statistics 2001, volume 4* (for Chile, Hong Kong [China], Hungary, Thailand) and from Laboursta (for Australia, Malaysia, Paraguay, Switzerland, USA). Nevertheless, it has not been possible to obtain data for many poor countries, especially in sub-Saharan Africa.

In preparing chart 4, we were handicapped by the lack of new data for the following countries: **sub-Saharan Africa**-Burkina Faso, Cote d'Ivoire, Ethiopia, Kenya, Niger, Swaziland; **Central and Western Asia**-Jordan, Syria; **Asia and the Pacific**-Fiji, Indonesia, Malaysia, Pakistan; **Latin America and the Caribbean**-Bahamas, Barbados, El Salvador, Honduras, Jamaica; **Eastern Europe**-Albania; **Western Europe and Other Developed Countries**-Austria. The data for the mid 1990s for these countries is taken from Table 4, *Progress of the World's Women 2000*.

GENDER EQUALITY IN POLITICAL PARTICIPATION

Table 7 shows women's share of seats in the national parliament and changes in this share are shown in Chart 5. The data is taken primarily from the Inter-Parliamentary Union (IPU) website for 1 July 2002 and 25 January 2000. The data for 2000 are taken from Human Development Report 1999 table 3, pp.142-44 for the following countries: **sub-Saharan Africa**-Botswana, Togo; **Asia and the Pacific**-Indonesia, Pakistan, Thailand; **Latin American and the Caribbean**-Panama.

A number of countries have both upper and lower chambers of parliament (bicameral legislatures): **sub-Saharan Africa**-Burundi, Ethiopia, Gabon, Lesotho, Liberia, Madagascar, Mauritania, Namibia, Nigeria, South Africa, Swaziland; **North Africa**-

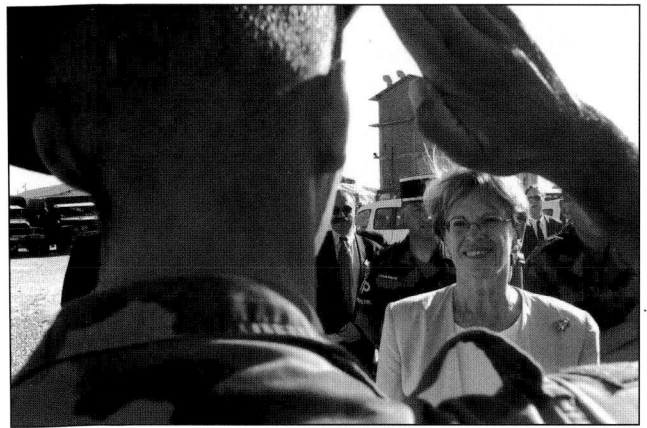

A French soldier salutes French Defense Minister Michelle Alliot-Marie in Kabul, 2002.

Algeria, Morocco; **Central and Western Asia**-Jordan, Kazakhstan, Kyrgyzstan, Tajikistan; **Asia and the Pacific**-Cambodia, Fiji, India, Malaysia, Nepal, Philippines, Thailand; **Latin America and the Caribbean**-Argentina, Barbados, Belize, Bolivia, Brazil, Chile, Colombia, Dominican Rep., Haiti, Jamaica, Mexico, Paraguay, Trinidad & Tobago, Uruguay; **Eastern Europe**-Belarus, Bosnia and Herzegovina, Croatia, Czech Rep., Hungary, Poland, Romania, Russian Fed., Yugoslavia FR; **Western Europe and Other Developed Countries**-Australia, Austria, Belgium, Canada, France, Germany, Ireland, Italy, Japan, Netherlands, Spain, Switzerland, United Kingdom, United States. In such cases, we follow the procedure used in the *Human Development Report*, and data in the table and chart for 2000 and 2002 usually refer to women's share of seats in the combined chambers (number of women in lower house plus number of women in upper house divided by total number of seats in lower house plus upper house). But note that shares for 2000 for Ethiopia, South Africa, Cambodia, Haiti and the United Kingdom are lower house while 2002 shares for all of these countries are combined (upper and lower houses). For Mauritania the share in 2000 is for combined houses, while for 2002 it is for the upper house. In a few cases, for the latest elections, only women's share of seats in the lower chamber is reported: Burundi and Madagascar in sub-Saharan Africa; Fiji and Nepal in Asia and the Pacific; Trinidad & Tobago in Latin America and the Caribbean. In some cases new election results were not reported in time for inclusion: Chad, Comoros, Libya, Sierra Leone in sub-Saharan and North Africa; Bahamas in Latin America and the Caribbean; and Vanuatu in Asia and Pacific.

Data for 1987 is taken from *The World's Women 1995: Trends and Statistics*, Table 14, pp.171-75, and includes data only for women's share of seats in the lower chamber of bicameral parliaments. The primary source of this data is IPU, *Distribution of Seats between Men and Women in the 144 National Assemblies*, Series Reports and Documents No. 14 (Geneva 1987).

REFERENCES

Anker, R. et al. 2002. *Measuring Decent Work with Statistical Indicators.* Policy Integration Paper No. 1, Statistical Development and Analysis Unit, Policy Integration Department. Geneva: ILO.

Banerjee, Nirmala. 2000. *Poverty and Social Development.* Paper presented at seminar on Poverty and Development, Centre for Studies in Social Sciences, Calcutta, India.

Budlender, Debbie, Diane Elson, Guy Hewitt and Tani Mukhopadhyay. 2002. *Gender Budgets Make Cents: Understanding Gender Responsive Budgets.* London: Commonwealth Secretariat.

Carlsson, Helene and Cecilia Valdivieso. 2003. *Gender Equality and the Millennium Development Goals.* Gender and Development Group, Washington, DC: World Bank.

Economic Commission for Latin America and the Caribbean (ECLAC). 2002a. 'ECLAC and the Millennium Development Goals,' note prepared for international seminar, 'Latin America and the Caribbean: Challenges of the Millennium Development Goals.' IDB/World Bank/UNDP/ECLAC. Washington DC, June.
_____. 2002b. *Demographic Bulletin*, special issue on Gender Sensitive Indicators, July.

FLACSO. 2003. (forthcoming). *Index of Fulfilled Commitments*, Santiago, Chile.
_____. 2001. *Index of Fulfilled Commitments*, Santiago, Chile.

Grown, Caren, Geeta Rao Gupta and Zahia Kahn. 2003. "Promises to Keep: Achieving Gender Equality and the Empowerment of Women: A Background Paper for the Task Force on Education and Gender Equality of the Millennium Project." International Center for Research on Women (ICRW). Washington, D.C.

International Labour Organization (ILO). 2002a. *Women and Men in the Informal Economy: A Statistical Picture, Employment Sector.* Geneva: ILO.
_____. 2002b. In Focus Programme on Social-Economic Security, Newsletter 1. Geneva: ILO.

Ruiz Abril, Maria Elena. 2003. 'Challenges and Opportunities for Gender Equality in Latin America and the Caribbean.' Washington, DC: World Bank.

Social Watch. 2002. Social Watch Report

2002. Institut de Tercer Mundo, Montevideo: Uruguay.

UN. 2001. *Beijing and Beyond.* New York: UN Division for the Advancement of Women.
———. 1995. *The World's Women 1995: Trends and Statistics.* 2nd ed. New York: UN Statistical Division.

UNDP. 2002. *Human Development Report 2002.* New York: Oxford University Press.

UNDP/UNICEF. 2002. "The Millennium Development Goals in Africa: Promises and Progress", Report prepared at the request of G-8 Personal Representatives for Africa. New York.

UNIFEM. 1997. "ACC Task Force on Basic Social Services for All: Guidelines on Women's Empowerment," UNIFEM: New York.
———. 2000. *Progress of the World's Women 2000.* New York: UNIFEM.
———. 2002. *Gender Budget Initiatives: Strategies, Concepts and Experiences.* New York: UNIFEM.